COLLECTOR'S ENCYCLOPEDIA OF

Blue Ridge DINNERWARE

VOLUME II

AN ILLUSTRATED VALUE GUIDE

BETTY & BILL NEWBOUND

COLLECTOR BOOKS
A Division of Schroeder Publishing Co., Inc.

The current values in this book should be used only as a guide. They are not intended to set prices, which vary from one section of the country to another. Auction prices as well as dealer prices vary greatly and are affected by condition and demand. Neither the Authors nor the Publisher assumes responsibility for any losses which might be incurred as a result of consulting this guide.

Searching For A Publisher?

We are always looking for knowledgeable people considered experts within their fields. If you feel that there is a real need for a book on your collectible subject and have a large comprehensive collection, contact Collector Books.

ON THE COVER:

Plate, Colonial shape, "Symmetry" pattern, $15.00 – 22.00.
China teapot, Colonial shape, "Rose Marie" pattern, $95.00 – 125.00.
Bud Top shakers with Good Housekeeping mark, $45.00 – 50.00 pair.

Cover Design: Beth Summers
Book Layout Design: Karen Geary

Additional copies of this book may be ordered from:

Collector Books
P.O. Box 3009
Paducah, KY 42002-3009

@ $24.95. Add $2.00 for postage and handling.

CONTENTS

ACKNOWLEDGMENTS AND THANKS

We have many people to thank this time since the book turned out to be more a joint effort than in the past, with help from many collectors over the country. Special and heartfelt thanks go to the following folks who loaned us dishes (and unfortunately lost some of them in the process), entertained us in their homes, sent hundreds of photos and certainly reinforced our conviction that collectors are the best people in the world!

Ray and Mary Farley, Norma and Sherman Lilly, Lawrence and Mary Lou Page, Bobby and Brenda Dowis, Jimmie Phelps, Emily and Jerry Gordon, Ralph Grissom, Elizabeth and Harold Ginsberg, Don and Susan Burkett, Katharine and Lewis Lilly, Dorothy Stratton, Eileen Jones, Evelyn Franklin, Lois and Lola Johnson, Frances Kyker Treadway, Rosmae Rowland, Jay Parker, and Kent Lee.

And to all the generous folks who sent us photos, many of which are used in this book… thank you all so very much!

Lewann Sowersby, Becky Denny, Terri Frantzen, Mickey Lohr, Karen Schultz, Julie Haben, Judy Simes, Julie Moessner, Ken Crossno, Mike and Marie Compton, Richard Brubaker, JoAnn Vidulich, Philip Shurley, Carol and Larry Southerland, Patricia Burghorn, Katie Pcenicne, Nancy Shuler, Pam Cook, Kathy Dougen, Jack and Maxine Looney, Annette Austin, Shirley and Bob Bond, Carl T. Booker, Mark Farison and Janet King-Farison, Chris Saari, Kim Austin, Jewel Barney, Sandra Barefoot, Elaine Rogers, Mary Linder, Sharon Riehl, Amy Irwin, Donna Eatmon, Lee Frye Burrow, Rosalie Tangen, Cynthia Norton, Shirley Hanson, Barbara Mandro-Lewis, Madelyn Kimmel Halley, Rhonda Reincke, Trudy Menzzentto, Jeannette Racette, Buddy Street, Richard Freed, Glen and Willene Clark, Bill Blumer, Fred Peister, Dwayne and Shirley Schramm, Cathy Cuddleford, and Eleanor Clouse Fondren.

Thank you…thank you…we love you all.

FINDING FRIENDS AND GETTING HELP

THE NATIONAL BLUE RIDGE NEWSLETTER
Norma Lily, 144 Highland Dr.
Blountville, TN 37617
6 issues a year

BLUE RIDGE COLLECTOR'S CLUB
c/o Wanda Hashe
208 Harris St.
Erwin, TN 37650
This is a local club; one must be a member to attend the preview sale
the evening before the annual Blue Ridge Show and Sale.

SOUTHERN POTTERIES BLUE RIDGE DINNERWARE
by Bill and Betty Newbound
159 pgs., over 650 patterns, all color
$14.95 plus $2.50 postage

COLLECTOR'S ENCYCLOPEDIA OF BLUE RIDGE
by Bill and Betty Newbound
175 pgs., approximately 700 other patterns, all color
$19.95 plus $2.50 postage

Order books from authors at 4567 Chadsworth, Commerce, MI 48382
or
Collector Books, Box 3009, Paducah, KY 42001

HISTORY

Picture a small southern town, nestled in a deep valley near the crest of the Blue Ridge Mountains. The time is 1917 and an event is taking place that will change the town and its people immensely. A pottery has been built, along with about 40 company houses for pottery workers, and when the train arrives, townfolk will turn out to welcome several dozen skilled pottery tradesmen and their families who have come from established pottery country in Ohio and Virginia to work in E. J. Owens' brand new Clinchfield Pottery.

At the turn of the century, you understand, America's railroads did not depend simply on carrying freight and passengers from place to place. They also bought land and developed, or helped develop, industries along their lines to ensure having plenty of business in the future. It was the Carolina, Clinchfield and Ohio Rail-road's Holston Corporation that sold the land for the pottery in Erwin, Tennessee. I wonder if Mr. Owens could possibly have foreseen his pottery growing into the largest hand-painted dinnerware plant in the nation, producing some 24 million pieces yearly. Probably he did not, because Clinchfield Pottery started out using a standard decal decorating concept and was only mildly successful in its first few years.

The pottery name was changed in 1920 when, on April 8th, a charter was issued to Southern Potteries, Incorporated. After a few years, the plant was purchased by Charles W. Foreman, an associate of Mr. Owens from their former Ohio pottery years. Mr. Foreman brought with him the technique of hand painting under the glaze, and from then on, the tide turned for Southern Potteries. Girls and women from the area were trained in the freehand paint-

Town of Erwin, Tennessee, nestled in a valley of the Blue Ridge Mountains.

ing techniques and the quality of workmanship improved continually.

This fresh, uninhibited approach, combined with a spectrum of bright, clear colors, was a welcome innovation in the world of mainly decal decorated dinnerware with its necessarily rigid and uniform styling, and became an immediate hit. By 1938, Southern Potteries had evolved to a full hand-painting operation and "Blue Ridge Hand-Painted Under the Glaze Dinnerware" was well established.

Southern Potteries expanded enormously until by the mid 1940s and early 1950s, over one thousand workers were producing more than 324,000 pieces of decorated ware each week. This was sold by all means, from a large national sales organization to traveling men with small trucks who served Mom and Pop stores throughout the South and Midwest.

The plant included scores of potters wheels for flatware and a casting department for hollow ware. There were finishing and stamping departments, five huge kilns, a barrel-making department and a section where the frit or glaze was produced. Besides these, there were a storage area, a shipping department, a warehouse, and a section that produced the basic raw material used to make the clay bodies. Add to these the usual executive, clerical, sales and bookkeeping departments and you will understand the size of this operation.

By the mid 1950s, Southern Potteries found themselves fighting to stay afloat in a new world of postwar imports, rising salaries, and plastic dinnerware. Despite all their efforts, the plant was finally closed on January 31, 1957, and the remaining stockholders paid off. Only the central core of the old pottery building remains today. The workers' homes have long since been sold to other individuals and blended into the fabric of the town. It was truly the end of an era, and Erwin will always remember the "glory days" when Southern Potteries was the best in the nation.

See *Southern Potteries Blue Ridge Dinnerware* and the *Collector's Encyclopedia of Blue Ridge* for more comprehensive history and photos of pottery production work.

Dump behind the old Southern Potteries plant.

SURVEYING THE MARKET

During the almost 17 years since *Southern Potteries Blue Ridge Dinnerware* was published, we have come to see a definite pattern emerging in the collecting of Blue Ridge. Folks love and look for the fancy china (or porcelain) pieces; pitchers, boxes, trays, teapots, chocolate pots, vases, etc. Charm House china pieces are very popular, but elusive. Hard to find and expensive are the Sherman Lily Box, the Dancing Nudes box, Mallard box, and the Chocolate Tray along with the complete Lazy Susan set which oddly enough is *not* porcelain.

In rarity, the artist-signed pieces head the list with the big Wild Turkey platter and the Turkey Gobbler platter along with its matching plate and cup being most difficult to locate. Please remember that artist-signed pieces are always signed on the *front* of the piece. Backstamps such as "Dorothy Bon-bon" are shape names, not artist names. Next come the Character Jugs. Of the four, Paul Revere seems the most elusive followed by the Indian.

Sample marked pieces are a plum in any collection (see Sample section, p. 20), along with the Designer Series of fantastically-patterned plates that probably never got into regular production because they did not sell at the dinnerware shows. Patterns in the Designer Series included Kaleidoscope, Dragon Song, Fanciful, Abracadabra, and Mosaic. (See *Southern Potteries Dinnerware*, page 44.)

The various children's pieces either in sets or separately are probably next in popularity and scarcity, closely followed by the Christmas and Thanksgiving patterns such as "Christmas Tree," "Christmas Doorway" (the more elusive of the two), "Holly," "Poinsettia," "Thanksgiving Turkey," and "Turkey With Acorns." Next in line are the little 5½" square plates of the "Country Life" series.

Advertising pieces are sought by many collectors today. These consist of everything from the Blue Ridge Counter Sign to the large palette-shaped plates featuring Blue Ridge Dinnerware, Primrose China, and Talisman Wallpaper. Also in this category are the many ashtrays, plates, and pitchers printed with advertising and/or holiday greetings from various businesses.

The most highly-prized pattern in regular dinnerware was and still is "French Peasant," followed closely by the Provincial Line designs. (See more about the Provincial Line, p. 97.) The eight-piece Songbird pattern salad sets in Aster, Skyline, and Colonial shapes are extremely desirable and avidly hunted. Next in popularity are any patterns depicting people, boats, birds, and chickens along with farm or cabin scenes such as "Eventide," "Red Barn," and "Weather-vane." Vegetable-patterned pieces have surfaced over the last couple of years and are also eagerly hunted.

The five patterns that Southern Potteries made in the early 1950s to match Talisman wallpaper may well turn out to be very rare patterns in dinnerware. These are Cherry Time, Woodbine, Talisman Wild Strawberry, Yorktown, and Blossom Tree. The idea was evidently not too successful and not many pieces were made. Woodcrest was another idea that did not find favor with the buying public and consequently any Woodcrest patterns are in rather short supply.

Many collectors find figural Mallard duck and the many-colored chicken shakers fantastic additions to their collections and their prices have steadily climbed over the years. Teapots, coffee pots, and demitasse sets have quite a following, along with the Betsy Jugs and the Carafe. Remember that teapots and fancy pitchers can be found in both china (porcelain) *and* earthenware (semi-porcelain). Large salad bowls with underplates and the television-inspired snack sets are also very popular and rising in price.

In sets, the eleven-piece Breakfast Set and the fifteen-piece Children's Play Set are elusive and costly. The eight-piece salad plate sets in both 8½" round and the smaller 5¾" square versions are next in line with the "Language of Flowers," the "Mandarin Series," the "Mexico Lindo," "Caribbean," and the "Songbird" sets commanding the highest prices.

Not to be ignored are the gorgeous painted plates that abound in Blue Ridge. Collectors hunt these and use them as works of art on their walls and plate rails and inside their glass-fronted cabinets. Folks especially look for the larger 10" plates and for highly decorated platters.

We are really pleased to notice at shows, malls, and markets how many young people are starting collections. They are enthusiastic hunters and want not only the dishes but also all the information about them they can. This bodes very well for the future of Blue Ridge collecting into the next century.

THE EARLY YEARS
CLINCHFIELD CHINAWARE

In the past year or two, we have seen an increase in the number of collectors of early Southern Potteries ware, known as Clinchfield Chinaware. This was produced from about 1918 to 1920 until hand painting took over completely in 1938. On April 20, 1930, the *JOHNSON CITY CHRONICLE AND STAFF-NEWS* presented a double page advertisement for "Southern Potteries Incorporated—Manufacturers of Clinchfield Chinaware." One page showed a number of views of the inside and outside of the pottery. The other page contained a selection of dishes illustrating a few of the available decals and shapes. "Clinchfield on china is like Sterling on silver," the ad proclaimed. Also mentioned were "A full and complete line of popular-priced salad bowls" and "Dinner ware; plain white, gold decorations, floral decorations." Listed too were the names of the raw material suppliers for Southern Potteries with "Only the best from the markets of the world."

At this time, decals were purchased from the same suppliers by many different potteries and you are likely to find the same decals on pieces made by several different companies. Several of the decorations featured in this ad are the Bluebird pattern, Godey Ladies and Dutch Mother and Child. Salad bowls were sold separately as well as plates advertised as Souvenir Plaques that could be imprinted on the front or back with a company's advertising message. Shapes in the dinnerware shown are Clinchfield, which carried over into the early days of hand painting, and Watauga, which looks just slightly twelve-sided. Among "old shapes" from the decal days carried over into the hand-painting era were "Waffle," "Rib," and "Scalloped Beading."

The bulk of the decal-decorated Clinchfield Chinaware does not vary greatly from the output of any of the hundreds of other potteries operating at that time. However, there are facets of the production that can be interesting and make a nice addition to the Blue Ridge collection. Some of the decal-decorated pieces were quite elaborate with wide colored borders surrounding the central motif and covered with intricate patterns in gold. Often these will carry on the reverse side the National Brotherhood of Operative Potters stamp. Or you might find an advertising or special order message such as one we have seen bearing "Compliments of Frank T. Gentry, Superintendent of Schools, Unicoi County, December 1941." This piece was also marked "Southern Potteries Inc., Warranted gold 22Kt. Made in U.S.A."

Of interest also are the animal figures made by Southern Potteries around 1932–1933. We have heard of many different animal figures, but so far we have found very few that are authenticated. The word "authenticated" is, as the old-timers say, "the clod in the churn" as far as collecting the animals. Very, very few were marked in any way, and since practically every pottery in business at the time made some sort of animal figurine and none was at all adverse to copying from one another, it is very difficult to be sure your animal is a Southern Potteries product. The animals were decorated by the air-brush method, since this was before the time of hand painting at Southern.

Some of the early Clinchfield pieces were covered entirely with an orange luster, looking almost Japanese. These luster pieces make a fine addition to an Early Years collection, but are a challenge to find.

There seems to be some confusion about decorating methods in the older chinaware. Seems that Transfer, Stencil, Stamp, and Decal are being used interchangeably by a lot of folks when they are totally different methods.

Rubber stamps very much like the stamps we use at our desks were used mainly for the backstamp or trademark on the backs of our dishes. They were also used for gold decoration, using liquid gold instead of the usual ink. Sometimes stamps were made large enough to form the whole central design on a dish or made in sections to form border patterns. Stamped lines are not as clear and sharp as decal lines. Familiar edge treatments on Blue Ridge were often done with a sponge stamp. A relatively flat surface is necessary for a stamp to work well. Stamped designs are usually one color, but were sometimes embellished with hand-painted touches.

Transfers have the designs printed on tissue paper. Some potteries buy transfers dry in sheets; some print them right in the pottery decorating shop. When the transfer is made at the pottery, the design is printed on an offset press with a heavy application of slow-drying ink. The decorators then cut out the designs and lay them on the piece to be decorated with the ink turned against the bisque ware. The transfer is then carefully rubbed so the ink is absorbed by the bisque. Using a little water, the tissue is scrubbed off, leaving the design. If hand tinting is needed, it is done next, then the piece is glazed and fired. If dry transfers are used, it is necessary to coat the item to be decorated with varnish to provide a tacky surface for the pattern. The item is then run through the decorating kiln to burn out oils and impurities and set the pattern. Glaze is applied, followed by another firing.

Decals were a big business in the earlier china days; almost everybody used them to some extent. They were just about the same as the decals you can buy in the shops now. Using gummed paper, a printing press prints the design *area* on the gummed side in varnish instead of ink. Then, the colored design itself is printed so that it falls on top of the previously printed varnish. The varnish area makes a base for the colors, which are printed with ceramic inks. The decals are then cut into units. To use, the decal is placed in water to soften the gum. Then the design is slid off the paper on its film of varnish and placed on the pottery, either bisque or glazed. Decorating over the glaze was a cheaper method which eliminated at least one firing; however, the decorations did not wear well.

The old Clinchfield Chinaware was mainly decal decorated, while the later Blue Ridge patterns that used the outline and fill-in method of decorating were basically rubber stamps with hand coloring. Actually, the word "stencil" is a misnomer to a great extent since that method was very seldom used on pottery.

As far as the marks on early Clinchfield Chinaware go, you will find that almost always the word "Southern" or the initials "S.P.I." will be found incorporated into the Clinchfield mark. All this sounds simple enough, doesn't it? The confusion comes when folks find pieces of Clinchfield Artware pottery, which was also made in Erwin, but by the Cash Family. The words to remember are "Artware" and "Cash Family." If these words are present, the item is *not* a Southern Potteries product. See further information on the Cash Family Pottery elsewhere in this book.

Decal and gold decorated plate on Candlewick shape, "Black Beauty."

Left: "Stately." Right: "First Class." Both bear Clinchfield crown mark.

Left:
"Basket," 11⅝" platter, crown mark.

Right:
"Poppy," 10⅝" platter, crown mark.

Left:
6" plate, marked NASCO, LA ROSE, along with crown mark.

Right:
6" plate, "Janice," Trellis shape; crown mark.

12" platter, "Crest" pattern on Clinchfield shape.

"Empress" plate on Candlewick shape.

Crusader Series: "March Through the Desert."

Crusader Series: "The Defender of The Cross."

All of the Crusader Series plates are marked with the Clinchfield crown mark plus the words "Van Dyne" in gold.

Crusader Series: "Converted to the Christian Faith."

Crusader Series: "The Arrival Before Jerusalem."

All of the Crusader Series plates are marked with the Clinchfield crown mark plus the words "Van Dyne" in gold.

Crusader Series: "Offering of Prayer After the Battle."

Crusader Series: "A Dangerous Intruder."

Confederate Monument plate, Stone Mountain, Ga. Shown are Robert E. Lee, Stonewall Jackson, and Jefferson Davis on horseback. There are troops in the background that do not appear on the actual monument.

"Eden" bowl, crown mark.

"Solitary Rose" bowl on the Watauga shape, crown mark.

"Fabulous," 10½" oval bowl, Watauga shape, crown mark.

11¾" covered vegetable, #226, Watauga shape, crown mark.

"Snowflake," 9½" squared bowl, rib shape.

"Yellow Tea Rose," 10¾" bowl, crown mark.

Maria" bowl, crown mark.

"Steamer" bowl, crown mark.

THE DECORATORS

Southern Potteries was a huge operation in its heyday and certainly there were lots of jigger-men, cup handlers, mold makers, and kiln loaders among the nearly 1,000 workers, but the heart and soul of the pottery were the 500 or so decorators. Most were local girls and women who came to Southern Potteries to be trained in the art of folk painting. The decorating shop foreman would take a group of girls into the decorating department and teach them the basic strokes of folk painting. After a few hours, they were given simple patterns to copy and the most talented started work the same day, filling in details such as stems and leaves. Imagine 500 girls under a huge sawtooth roof — laughing, talking, brushes flying — creating colorful and sometimes fantastic flowers, fruits and birds on some 324,000 pieces of dinnerware a week! Some of the girls were true artists, some were just doing a job, but each put a little bit of themselves into every piece.

Work was done in crews of two to four girls, each concentrating on a certain part of the pattern. The girls changed jobs frequently to avoid monotony and keep a fresh approach. Most patterns were done purely freehand which accounts for the fascinating little changes we find when a number of plates of the same pattern are displayed together. Here is a bud that is not repeated on its sister plate — or one leaf instead of two. Or perhaps the flowers are larger on one plate than on another. Sometimes a girl would add a personal little squiggle to a flower, marking it as her work. All these little differences contribute to the charm that makes this handwork so appealing to collectors today.

Nearly all the thousands (yes, thousands!) of patterns used by Southern Potteries originated at the pottery. Lena Watts was head designer for a number of years, along with designing and decorating at Clouse Pottery, also located in Erwin. (See section on Clouse, p. 219.) Lena's scenic plates with lonely cabins and mills; her varied wildlife scenes and huge turkey platters are outstanding examples of American folk art. In later years, Lena left Southern Potteries to take employment at Stetson China Company in Lincoln, Illinois. Rosmae Rowland took her place at Southern and designed for about the last 10 years of Southern Potteries' existence.

Exclusive patterns were often created through teamwork between the buyer for a large department or mail-order store and Southern's designer. Colors were carefully chosen with close attention to color trends in women's and home fashions. Stores like Sears Roebuck & Co. and Montgomery Ward often requested use of their own colors. Obtaining the color pigments and getting them to fire properly were big problems and took many hours of experimentation.

During the later years when Southern, along with many American potteries, was fighting for its life amid the growing post-war wave of cheap imports, rubber stamps were used to speed the decorating process. The girls filled in the outlines with paint, much like a child's coloring book. Many of these stamp and fill-in patterns are quite appealing, but the girls felt they weren't so artistic as the freehand designs.

Even though Southern Potteries has been closed for 40 years now, the annual Blue Ridge Show and Sale held in Erwin still brings out some of the ladies whose vocation was decorating the pottery. They often react with a mixture of surprise that "those old dishes" are now being loved and cherished by so many. We hear lots of stories from these ladies. "There was a box of cups to be decorated on the floor next to me," said one, "and one day I reached down and lifted a cup onto my table and there was a mouse in it! I screamed and threw that cup the whole length of the room!" "Sometimes the company let us decorate a piece or two for ourselves or for a special family occasion and we put our name or initials on the back so we could find it when it came out of the kiln," another lady told us. This explains the pieces we sometimes are lucky enough to find with that signature or initials on the back. (Keep in mind that these are *not* considered "artist signed" pieces. The signatures on artist-signed items are always on the front.)

The huge, bright, decorating department with the sawtooth roof is gone and the girls who painted there are white-haired ladies now, but the memory of the big room filled with rattling dishes, bright colors, and laughter still holds a special place in their hearts and in the hearts of the town. I think it holds a special place in the hearts of the collectors too!

See *Southern Potteries Blue Ridge Dinnerware* and *Collector's Encyclopedia of Blue Ridge* for more comprehensive information and photos.

ROSMAE ROWLAND

When Lena Watts left her head designer's post at Southern Potteries about 1946, the position was taken over by decorator Rosmae Rowland who continued as head designer until one year before Southern Potteries closed in 1957. Business was so bad, Rosmae said, there was no need for new patterns in that fateful year.

Rosmae traveled to many large stores with their own accounts, such as J. L. Hudson in Detroit, Michigan (where Bill and I bought our very first set), plus stores in Cincinnati and Cleveland, Ohio, among others. Rosmae stayed about two weeks at a place and would do painting exhibitions in the store and also on television. She told us "as long as I just painted and didn't have to talk, I'd do it."

At one point in her career, Rosmae was in the hospital and Southern desparately needed more new designs for an upcoming show, so they brought her supplies to the hospital and she did samples in watercolors right from her bed! Now there's a dedicated employee. Rosmae did some landscape painting with private lessons, she told us, but had no formal art training before she began at Southern Potteries.

FRANCES KYKER TREADWAY

This lady's name will be familiar to any collector lucky enough to own an artist-signed plate. Frances graduated from high school at

Frances Kyker Treadway

Rosmae Rowland

"Solitary Rose" bowl on the Watauga shape, crown mark.

"Fabulous," 10½" oval bowl, Watauga shape, crown mark.

11¾" covered vegetable, #226, Watauga shape, crown mark.

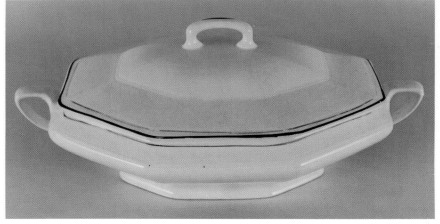

"Snowflake," 9½" squared bowl, rib shape.

"Yellow Tea Rose," 10¾" bowl, crown mark.

"Santa Maria" bowl, crown mark.

"Steamer" bowl, crown mark.

age 15, she told us, having received most of her education in one-room district schools. She skipped at least one grade because she would have been the only student in that grade and the teacher did not want to bother with a one-student class. She had no formal art training, just a natural talent. Frances decorated for Southern Potteries for 16 years, from 1941 to 1957.

When Frances started, girls had one day of practice on brush strokes and then were put on a crew doing various parts of patterns. Ten years later, she said, there was no practice day — girls just started in — which may account for some of the really poor work one sometimes finds on plates. Decorators were paid by the hour with a certain quota to fill. For anything done over that quota, they received a bonus.

There was no air-conditioning in those days, just lots of fans. The decorators sat at long benches and when Frances "graduated" to artist-signed pieces, she and the other artists were somewhat isolated at the end of a bench. She told us she could do six artist-signed Mill, Cabin, Quail or Turkey plates a day. Girls upstairs did decal and lining work when Southern was still producing that type of ware.

Mr. Forman, the owner, was not at the plant most of the time, but when he did come around, Frances said, the girls got rather apprehensive and were always afraid of dropping something.

On one such visit, a girl did drop a cup and everyone burst into nervous giggles. Mr. Forman said he "didn't mind the damn breakage," but he "hated the laughing about it!" Georgia Garvin, Frances' sister, also painted at Southern, and they traveled to work together.

Frances does not paint any more although she showed us a number of crocks and other small items she decorated for herself and family a few years ago. The talent is still there.

LENA WATTS

Lena was head designer at Southern Potteries from almost the beginning of hand painting until about 1946 when she left to accept a position at Stetson Pottery in Lincoln, Illinois. After that time, most Stetson ware began to look like Southern Potteries'. Although she did not have formal art training, she did have an outstanding eye for color and design. Lena also designed and painted for awhile with her sister, Bonnie Clouse, at Clouse's Unaka Pottery. She died on May 23, 1993, in Florida at age 91.

LOIS and LOLA JOHNSON

These diminutive twin sisters were a joy to talk to! They painted at Southern Potteries for 15 years, from 1942 to 1957. Although they had

Lena Watts in a playful mood.

Left to right: Lola and Lois Johnson

no formal art training, they painted the "Art Ware" which consisted of the china or porcelain pieces (chocolate pots, vases, boxes, etc.), the character jugs, and Charm House line. These items were painted entirely by one artist instead of the crew method used for regular dinnerware. Lois did Charm House pieces and told us that a higher grade of china was used for these pieces. Skin tones on the character jugs' faces were sprayed on, and the girls did the rest. Lois did almost all the Pioneer Women, she said, while Lola did the Indians. They could paint about 12 character jugs or Betsy Jugs a day. They assured us that there was only *one size* of these character jugs produced. They mentioned that when chicken and duck shakers were painted, a pencil or stick was inserted in the hole on the bottom so that the decorator's fingers did not smear the paint while holding onto the base. Each decorator owned her own brushes and was responsible for them. Lois talked about losing a whole day's work when the 12 chocolate pots she had completed were dropped on the floor by the boy carrying them to the transport cart. "All he had to do," she said, "was put them on a board, turn around, and put it on the cart, but he tilted the board just a little too much and down they went." After Southern Potteries closed, the twins worked part-time for awhile at Cash's Clinchfield Artware Pottery in Erwin. Some of the painting work they did at home. Today, 40 years after Southern Potteries closed, they are still painting lovely plates which they sell from a local gift shop.

SAMPLE PIECES

All sample-marked pieces are avidly hunted by Blue Ridge collectors and that fact is reflected in the prices one finds at shows and malls. Sample pieces show the pattern number; remember, Southern Potteries used only numbers, not names, for their patterns unless they were nationally advertised. They generally have the "Sample Approved" stamp and the names of the colors used in the pattern. This information was on the front or top of the piece unless the pattern was so intricate or the piece so small that there was no room. In that case, you will find this information on the back.

When the head designer created a pattern, she had to keep track of the number of brush strokes necessary to complete it, and the number of colors and their names, such as dark blue, regular red, etc. After completing a few pieces, the item was submitted to management who examined the pattern and decided whether it could be made at a profit, considering carefully the cost of paint and number of man-hours (or in this case, woman hours) needed.

When the pattern was approved, a few pieces, perhaps a place setting or two, were made and exhibited at the big dinnerware shows held periodically around the country. Or they were shown to the buyers who visited Southern Potteries regularly. Sometimes a pattern just did not sell and was summarily discontinued and the display pieces sold as seconds. This results in collectors sometimes finding a plate or two for a certain pattern and then never finding another piece. If a pattern did sell, enough pieces were made so that each girl on the crew could have one to copy. In the warehouse photo in *Collector's Encyclopedia of Blue Ridge,* you can see hundreds of sample plates hanging on the back wall just waiting to be needed.

"Nesting Birds" platter.

"Chicken Pickins" plate.

Left: "Likeness" or "Eglantine" may have begun with this 10" plate. Right: "Country Strawberry," 10" plate.

"Nola" (left); "Nocturne" (right).

7" plate; probably painted by Allene Miller.

Quarter-pound butterdish.

Left:
Gene Kyle shaker, sample #3634.

Right:
Skyline shaker, sample #4120.

"Apple Pan Dowdy" bowl.

6⅜" diameter "Paint Sample" plate from B.F. Drakenfeld, liquid underglaze colors.

MOLD MAGIC

Mold making for china and pottery is an interesting occupation and while in Erwin some time ago, Bill took lessons in the art from a very fine and talented gentleman, John Hampton, who was for many years Southern Potteries' top mold maker. Besides learning the basics of mold making, Bill heard a lot of interesting facts about the origin of some of our best-loved Southern Potteries pieces. Southern had their own designer of original decorations and patterns, but like most all potteries of the time, many mold shapes were copies of something else. The mold for our lovely china chocolate pot was made from an antique silver pot. Several of our fancy pitcher shapes were copies of antique pitchers. Even the Character Jugs were not original with Southern Potteries. The set was brought to the mold maker, he tells us, and he was asked to copy them. Unfortunately, he did not remember any maker's mark in the originals.

If you look through greenware shops in the Erwin area, you will see copies of the Character Jugs as well as pitchers and some of the animals that were made by Southern Potteries back when they still used the Clinchfield name. We know, of course, that the Cash Family Pottery produced some of these pieces, but so far all have had their own mark on the bottom. The Erwin Pottery is currently producing reproductions of Southern Pottery pieces, not always with the Erwin mark.

To make sure we have a Southern Potteries piece, we must first check the mark. If there is none, we must look at the style and quality of the decoration. Also, the variance in formulas used in producing the clay bodies will cause the finished product to be slightly different in size than the Southern Potteries original. Character Jugs by Southern are somewhat smaller than those of the Cash Family because Southern used a fine china or porcelain base that shrinks more in firing than does the presently-used clay. So do your detective work before you buy an unmarked china piece. Remember, an experienced mold maker can make a mold from *any* existing pottery piece.

DINNERWARE SHAPES

There are 12 different shapes in which you will find Blue Ridge dinnerware. They are:
Candlewick: Beaded edge
Colonial: Fluted edge
Skyline: Sleek and plain
Skyline Studioware: Plain flatware with larger hollow ware pieces
Piecrust: Crimped edge
Clinchfield: Wide, flat rim
Astor: Narrow, slightly cupped rim
Trailway: Plain flatware with rope handled hollow ware
Woodcrest: Textured surface treatment
Monticello (Waffle): Border of incised squares
Palisades: Sleek and futuristic; tab points often on flatware
Trellis: Border of vertically fluted spaces between areas of cross-hatching.

Besides these dinnerware shapes, there are a number of different blanks that were used for the myriad "salad bowls" put out during the early Clinchfield Pottery era. Some of these shapes were continued into the hand-painting period which began about 1938, so they may be found decorated either with decals or with hand painting. These shapes include Wide Rib, Narrow Rib, Scalloped Beading, Lace Edge, Scroll Edge, Lotus Leaf, Squared Rib, Scallop, Yale, Square Round, and Curlicue Arch.

Square-shaped plates were mainly used as cake or salad plates and decorated to match whatever pattern the retailer selected. They are generally found in six, seven, and eight-inch sizes along with large, handled and squared cake plates.

So far, our research indicates that the Clinchfield shape was an early one, used in both decal production and hand painting. The large, artist-signed turkey platters and scenic cabin and mill plates are found on this shape.

The first three shapes produced in all hand painting were Candlewick, Astor, and Colonial. Advertisements show the "new" Piecrust shape in 1948 and Skyline in 1950. These were followed by Monticello (Waffle) and the highly textured

Woodcrest. Trailway, which is essentially Skyline flatware with rope handle and restyled flatware, was introduced about 1953. This was followed by the very modernistic Palisades shape and about this same time, Skyline was restyled using pretty much the same flatware, but changing the hollow ware pieces. This was dubbed Skyline Studioware.

The changes in Skyline, Skyline Studioware, and Trailway are confusing to collectors because the flatware remains basically the same in all three, making it necessary to acquire at least some of the sugars, creamers or cups in order to tell the pattern's category.

Also during the 1950s, a line of ovenware was introduced which included covered bowls, batter sets, ramekins, pie bakers, leftover dishes, and rectangular baking dishes. Markings of "Oven Proof" in the familiar Southern Potteries script will be found, along with the ovenware backstamps illustrated in the chapter on marks in this book. Some pieces were not marked at all and some will be found with a jobber's logo.

Keep in mind that the same pattern can and probably will be found on several different shapes.

Piecrust edge.

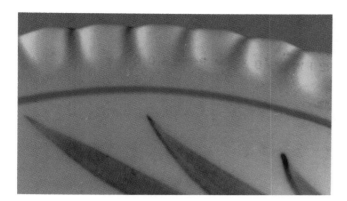

Candlewick edge.

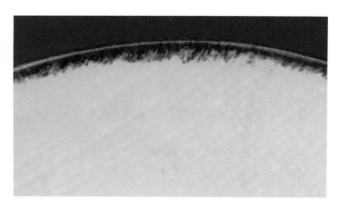

Woodcrest, textured.

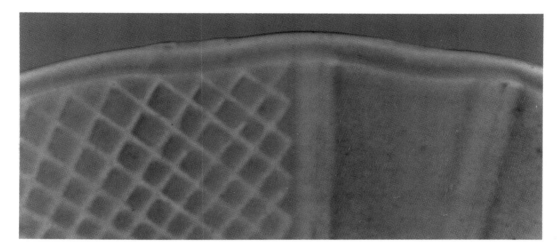

Trellis edge.

Colonial edge.

Clinchfield, wide edge.

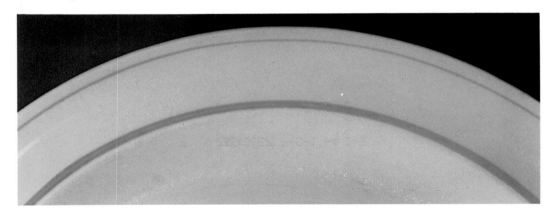

Astor, narrower cupped edge.

Skyline Studioware in "Roundelay" pattern.

Bottom view of "Leaf" flat cake plate.

"Leaf" flat cake plate.

Lotus Leaf edge.

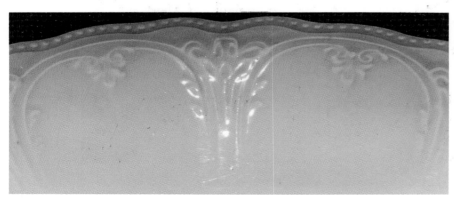

Curlicue Arch edge.

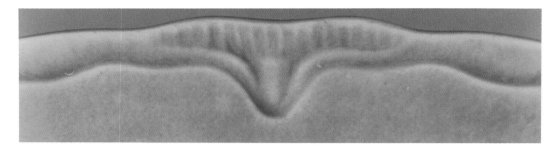

Lace edge.

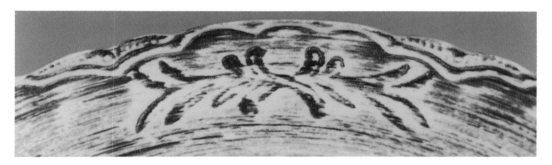

Scroll edge.

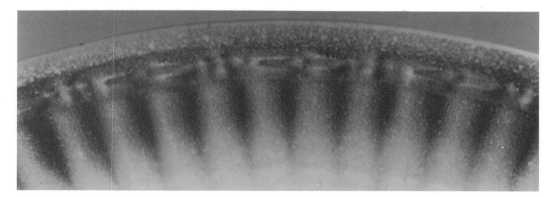

Squared Rib edge.

The lovely handle treatment on the Chocolate tray.

CUP SHAPES

Looking at the shape and the handle of your cups is the best way to decide whether or not the piece is indeed Blue Ridge and also to which blank or line it belongs. Southern made everything from the tiniest of demi cups to the huge Jumbo Cup and Saucer sets.

Trellis cup and saucer, "Daisy Chain" pattern.

Note the square base on the Woodcrest shape cups.

Astor cup and saucer, "Maude" pattern.

Top row: Colonial shape (left); "Turkey With Acorn Cup" (right).
Bottom row: Candlewick shape (left); Piecrust shape (right).

Top row: Trailway shape (rope handle) (left); Trellis shape (center); Woodcrest shape (right).
Bottom row: Square handle (left); Skyline shape (center); Astor shape (right).

Shows both sides of the "Christmas Doorway" cup.

This is a new shape we're occasionally running across. As yet unnamed, the pattern is "Ribbon Rose."

"Flower Bowl" demi cup and saucer, earthenware.

"Red Star" demi cup and saucer.

"Skeeter" demi cup and saucer marked with PV in a circle.

China demi cup and saucer, "Sweetheart Rose" pattern, marked Blue Ridge China and #18 in gold.

"French Peasant" in the heavier demi shape.

"Irish Mary" heavier demi cup.

"The Practical Pig" child's mug (also see Children's section.)

Child's mug in "Lyonnaise" pattern.

Jumbo cup in "Bulldog" pattern. This shows the entire cup.

Left: Same "Bulldog" with handle off.
Right: Same Jumbo cup showing the place where the handle slides in. Why this was done is a mystery. Was the cup just not finished? Was it somebody's idea that never took shape? Who knows?

Jumbo cup and saucer in "Lucky Find" pattern.

Two more Jumbo cups: "Beaded Chain" pattern (left); "Father" (right).

Jumbo cup and saucer in "Vonda" pattern.

Assortment of Provincial Line cups and saucers along with "Bulldog."

INTRODUCTION TO NEW PATTERNS

When we first began researching Blue Ridge, we discovered two things, much to our dismay. First, there were no written records left from Southern Potteries and second, there had never been any catalogs issued. Finally, we realized we would have to name most of the patterns ourselves, since Southern used almost entirely numbers which do not have much appeal. Unless patterns were nationally advertised by either Southern Potteries or the retailer, all names enclosed in quotation marks are ours and those suggested by loyal collectors everywhere.

Now and then you will find a single pattern with two different names. When this occurs it is usually the result of the "exclusive to area" agreement. This meant that Southern would sell a certain number of patterns to a store in, say, New York City. They would not sell these patterns to any other store in that area. However,

they would sell to a store in Cincinnati or Houston, for instance. Sometimes it would happen that both area stores would want to advertise the pattern and they would name it differently! Made sense at the time, but causes confusion to collectors today.

Speaking of confusion, one worry of ours was that someday other Blue Ridge books would come out and writers might name things differently. Well, it took awhile, but that very thing is happening now. From now on, if you are ordering or advertising by mail, you will have to be sure which reference book the advertiser is using. Keep in mind the alternate names (if any) for your patterns and save yourself disappointment and postage.

You will find this book presented differently from the past books. Here individual photos of patterns are pictured instead of shelves of pieces. This is because many kind and dedicated collectors furnished photos of their new patterns. Gone are the days when we could travel to one or two collectors and photograph 50 or 100 new patterns. There are still new patterns turning up all the time, but they are scattered over the country, two or three here, one there, a half-dozen somewhere else. We continue to be amazed that after the over 1,500 patterns shown in the previous books, we are still finding new treasures today. Will we ever find all Southern Potteries' prodigious output of designs? Probably not, but we thank for their help all the wonderful collectors whose names are listed elsewhere in this book. Please, keep hunting!

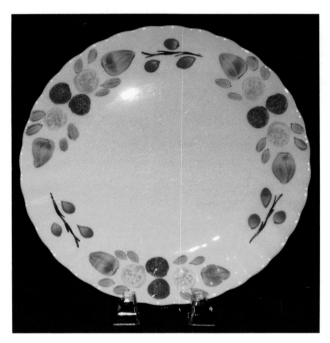

Colonial shape, "Gumdrop Wreath."

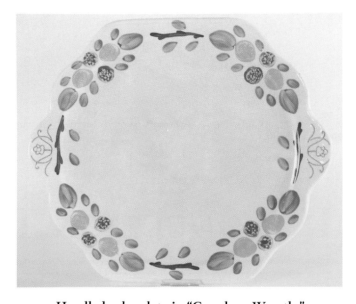

Handled cake plate in "Gumdrop Wreath."

Colonial shape, "Rural Retreat."

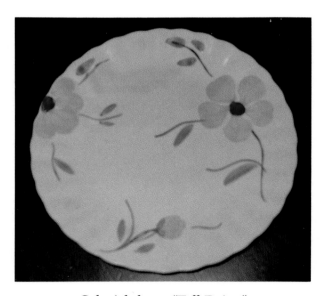

Colonial shape, "Fall Daisy."

Colonial shape, "Tess."

Colonial shape, "Garden Green."

Colonial shape, "One and Only."

Colonial shape, color variation of "Two-some."

Colonial shape, "Blarney."

Colonial shape, "Fuchsia."

Colonial shape, "Adalyn."

Colonial shape, "Brownfield," color variation of "Bluefield."

Colonial shape, "Wild Irish Rose," yellow color variation.

Colonial shape, "Johnny Jump-up."

Colonial shape plate and coupe soup, "Green Tornado."

Colonial shapes: "Florence" (left); "Jason" (right).

Colonial shapes: "Kim" (left); "Lavender Ruffles" (right).

Colonial shape, "Flower Meadow."

Colonial shape, "Mountain Daisy."

Colonial shape, "Pink Parfait."

Colonial shape, "Renee."

Colonial shape, "Texas Rose."

Colonial shape, "Star Gazer" (similar to "Starfire").

Colonial shape, 6" plates: "Glad Rags" (left), "Sprig" (right).

Colonial shape, "Vanity Fair."

Colonial shape, "Lea Marie."

Colonial shape:
"Janice" (left); "Blue Waves" (right).

Colonial shape platter, "In The Pink."

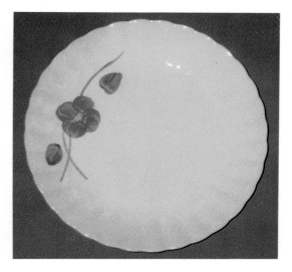

Colonial shape, "Meagan."

Colonial shape, "Autumn Berry."

Colonial shape, "Kennesaw."

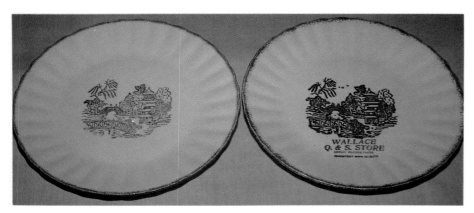

Colonial shape, "Ridge Blue Willow,"
Franklin Kent mark.

Colonial shape, "Simply Susan."

Colonial shape, "Cydney."

Colonial shape, "TopKnot."

Colonial shape, "Fall Garden."

Colonial shape bowl, "Queenie."

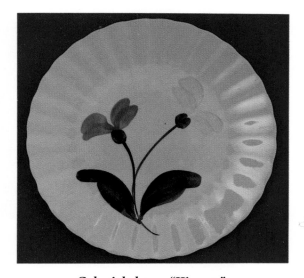

Colonial shape, "Kismet."

Colonial shape: "Mountain Crab" (left); "Amanda" (right).

Colonial shape, "Camelot."

Colonial shape, "Lovely Linda Variant."

Colonial shape, "Country Roadside."

Colonial shape, "Jonalyn."

Colonial shape, "Sheree."

Colonial shape, "Annabell."

Colonial shape, "Beverly."

Colonial shape, "Delightful."

Colonial shape, "Christmas Rose."

Colonial shape, "Vibrant."

Colonial shape, demi saucer, "Wiggle."

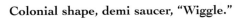

Colonial shape, "Red Velvet."

Colonial shape, "Symmetry."

Colonial shape: "Pine Mountain Tulip" (left); "Elsmere" (right).

Colonial shape, "Patsy Ann."

Colonial shape, "Leaf" variant.

Colonial shape: "Tillie" (left); "Green Apple" (right).

Colonial shape, "Red Maid."

Colonial shape, "Puritan."

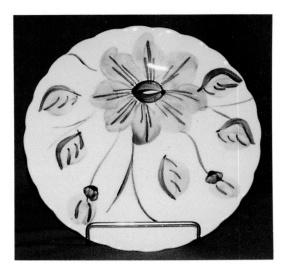

Colonial shape, "Blue Velvet."

Colonial shape, "Breath of Spring."

Colonial shape, "Carol's Corsage."

Colonial shape, "Kelci."

Colonial shape, "Extravaganza."

Cake plate, "Christmas Clover."

Colonial shape: "Madison" (left); "Pfiffle" (right).

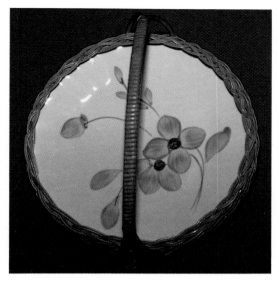

Colonial shape, "Pfiffle" pattern plate made into basket. The plate is placed inside wet wicker, and wicker shrinks to fit plate.

Colonial shape, "Arabella."

Colonial shape, "Beloved."

Colonial shape, "Erwin Spring."

Colonial shape, "Sutherland."

Colonial shape, "Fruitful."

Colonial shape, "Erwin."

Colonial shape, "Apple A Day."

Colonial shape, "Simply Sweet."

Clinchfield shape, "Late Bloomers."

Clinchfield platter, "Solidago."

Clinchfield shape, "Amy."

Clinchfield shape, "Ice Maiden."

Clinchfield shape, "Allison." (Same pattern in all yellow is "Mountain Daisy.")

Clinchfield shape, "Mountain Daisy."

Clinchfield plate, fork, and lifter in "Border Print."

Clinchfield shape, "Rowdy."

Clinchfield shape, "Shannon."

Clinchfield large platter, "Winter" (not artist-signed).

Clinchfield shape, "Tintagel." This is one of the designer patterns that may not have been put into production.

Clinchfield shape, artist-signed plates: "Yellow Cabin", signed Ruby S. Hart (left); "Flower Cabin," signed Frances Kyker (right).

This 12" "Shoveler Ducks" platter on Colonial shape is another piece the artist should have signed, but didn't. Possibly a sample from Southern's planned, but never produced, Audubon Bird line. Has Blue Ridge script mark and "Shoveler" on back.

Clinchfield shape, "Gold Cabin" (dark), signed Ruby S. Hart. Note that this "Gold Cabin" has a dark gold color background and the other, a lemon yellow background.

Clinchfield shape, "White Mill" plate, artist-signed by Nelsene Calhoun.

Clinchfield, "Thanksgiving Turkey on Sand." This platter is signed N. R. Webb. We understand that Webb was the maiden name of Negatha Peterson who paints the reproduction Blue Ridge and owns Erwin Pottery. Evidently this piece was painted when she worked at Southern.

Clinchfield shape, "Turkey Gobbler," artist-signed by Mae Garland.

Clinchfield shape, "Dance of Dots," another designer pattern.

Clinchfield shape, "Ellie's Place."

Clinchfield shape, "Jesse."

Piecrust shape, "Ralph's Orchard."

Piecrust shape, "Bounteous."

Piecrust shape, "Jingle Bell Poinsettia."

Piecrust shape, coupe soup bowl, "Emlyn."

Piecrust shape, "Cabbage Rose."

Piecrust shape, "Boutonniere."

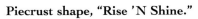

Piecrust shape, "Rise 'N Shine."

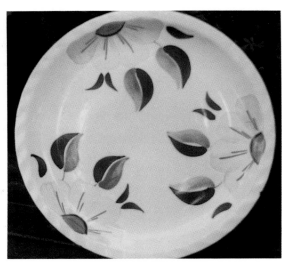

Piecrust shape, "Spring Blossom."

Piecrust shape, "Velma."

Woodcrest shape, "Little 'Uns." This is the party set, which is a plate with cup well and cup.

Woodcrest plate in the "Little 'Uns" pattern. Note variance in shape.

Woodcrest shape, "Strawberries Maxine."

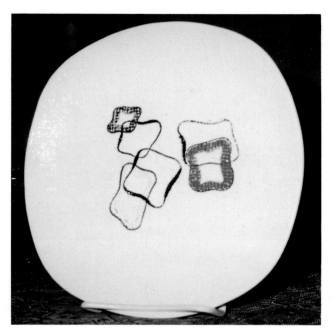

Woodcrest shape, "Square Meal."

Woodcrest shape, "Cactus."

Woodcrest shape, "Marlene."

Trailway shape, "Likeness."

Trailway shape, "Moss Rose." Also found in pink, brown, yellow color.

Trailway shape, "Flag Pond."

Trailway shape, "Tennessee Fruits."

Trailway cup and saucer, "Frolic." Note rope handle on cup. This is the distinguishing feature between Trailway and Skyline.

Trellis shape, "Richmond."

Trellis shape, "Happy Home."

Astor shape, "Pincushion."

Astor shape, "Maxine."

Astor shape, variation on plume, "Yellow Plume."

Astor shape, "Bluebonnet."

Astor shape, color variation of "Roseanne."

Astor shape, "Alicia."

Astor shape, "Sugar Run."

Astor shape, "Southern Rose."

Astor shape, "Pennsylvania Aster."

Astor shape, "Maude."

Astor shape, "Dungannon."

Astor shape, "October."

Astor shape, "Tulip Buds."

Astor shape platter, another variant of "Roseanne."

Astor shape, "Phlox."

Astor shape, "Tiger Eye."

Astor shape:
"Bluet" (left);
"Georgian Rose" (right).

Astor shape:
"Poetic" (left); "Stardust"
(right).

Astor shape, "Purple Passion."

Astor shape, "Chatelaine."

Astor shape, "Sue-Lynn."

Astor shape, "Wildlings."

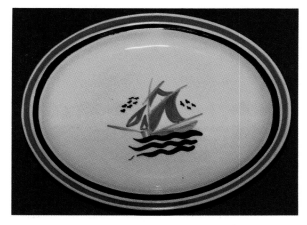

Astor shape, "Ship Ahoy."

Astor shape, "Tweet."

Astor shape, "Song Sung Blue."

Astor shape, "Strawberry Garden."

Astor shape, "Pearl."

Astor shape, "Tulip Corsage."

Astor shape, "Piquant."

Astor shape, "Scilla."

Astor shape, "Riotous."

Squared cake plate in "Riotous" pattern.

Astor shape, "Meredith."

Astor shape, "Mallow."

Astor shape, "Mistress Mary."

Astor shape, "Mexicano."

Candlewick shape, "Lizzie's Gift."

Candlewick shape, "Little Girl."

Candlewick shape, "Sensational."

Candlewick shape, "Ochoee."

Candlewick shape, "Victorian Rose."

Candlewick shape, "Kelvin."

Candlewick shape, Dana's Garden, SPI in diamond mark.

Candlewick shape, "Tulip Garden."

Candlewick shape, "Red Hill" variation.

Candlewick shape, "Precious."

Candlewick shape, "Jeanne."

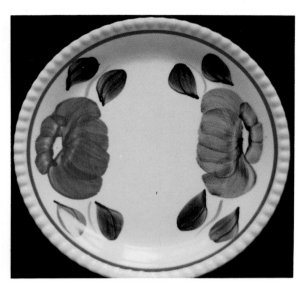

Candlewick shape, "Pom-pom."

Candlewick shape, "Twin Tulips."

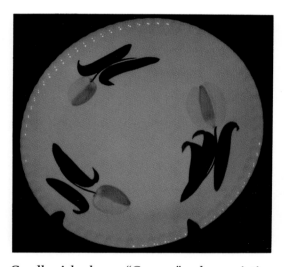

Candlewick shape, "Crocus," color variation of "Brownie."

Candlewick shape, "Maple Leaf Rag."

Candlewick shape, "Blossom Wreath."

Candlewick shape, "Kayla Ruth."

Candlewick shape, "Lorrie Dee."

Candlewick shape, "Verbena."

Candlewick shape, "Peggie's Posies" (Keillor).

Candlewick shape, "Caprice."

Candlewick shape, "Dorothy."

Candlewick shape:
"Starburst" (left);
"Signal Flags" (right).

Candlewick shape:
"Pink Mist" (left);
"Wee Flowers" (right).

Candlewick shape, "Blue Blossom." Note plate marked as such.

Candlewick shape, "Sylvia."

Candlewick shape, "Hydrangea."

Candlewick shape, "Hannah."

Candlewick shape, "Blue Mist."

Candlewick shape, "Starflower."

Candlewick shape, "Vida."

Candlewick shape, "Fountain Grass."

Candlewick shape, "Blue Rose."

Candlewick shape, "Ship Ahoy."

Candlewick shape, "Anne Elaine."

Candlewick shape, "Apple Pan Dowdy."

Candlewick shape, "Fruited Plain," 10" salad bowl. Matches salad set of same name.

Candlewick shape, "Golden Rays," plate signed "D. Hupp" on back.

Candlewick shape, "Candlewick Willow."

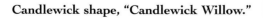

Candlewick shape, "Vegetable Soup."

Candlewick shape, "Chablis."

Candlewick shape, "Betty Mae."

Candlewick shape, "Yellow Dreams."

Candlewick shape, "Grandmother's Pride."

Candlewick shape, "Jonelle."

Candlewick shape, "Bronna."

Candlewick shape, "Luella."

Candlewick shape, "Paula's Lei."

Candlewick shape, "Samantha."

Candlewick shape, "Arlene With Leaf."
Pattern is also on Trellis shape with wide blue
border instead of leafy edge.

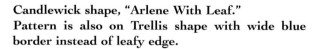

Skyline shape, "Grape Ivy."

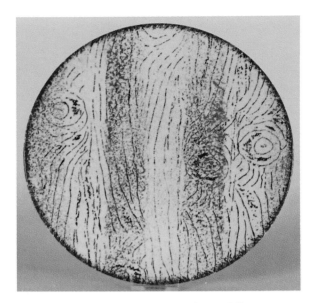

Skyline shape, "Birchwood."

Skyline shape, "Rocky Face."

Skyline shape, "Breakfast Bar" (Keillor).

Skyline shape, "Friendship Plaid."

Skyline shape: "Jungle Grass" (left); "Leaf & Circle" (right).

Skyline shape: "Roundelay" (left); "Scatter Plaid" (right).

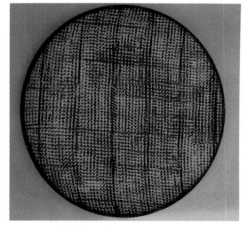

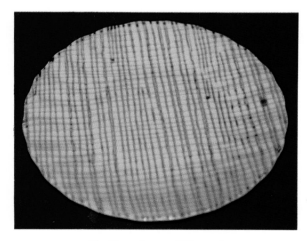

Skyline shape, "Curtis."   Skyline shape, "Linen."

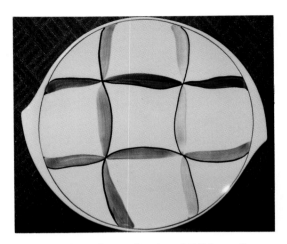

Skyline shape, "Twisted Ribbons."

Skyline shape, "Spring Beauty."

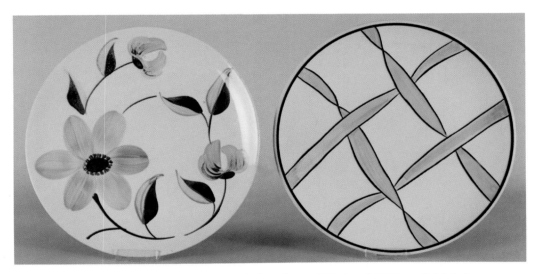

Skyline shape, "Bright Eyes" (left); "Pastel Twisted Ribbons" (right).

Skyline shape: "Midsummer Dream" (left); "Misty" (right).

Skyline shape, "Ashton."

Skyline shape, color variant of "Razzle Dazzle."

Skyline shape, "Orange Ice."

Skyline shape, "Brian."

Skyline shape, "Gloria Jean."

Skyline shape, "Butterfly Bouquet."

Skyline shape, "Spring Willow."

Skyline shape, "Chantilly."

Skyline shape, "Susan's Ring."

Skyline shape: "Lola" (left); "Lois" (right).

Skyline shape: "Ridge Ivy" (left); "Princess" (right).

Skyline shape: "Whirl" (left); "Rocky Face" (right).

Skyline shape, "Prim."   Skyline shape, "Pink Chiffon."

Skyline shape, "Tiny." Notice how small pieces have only part of the pattern.

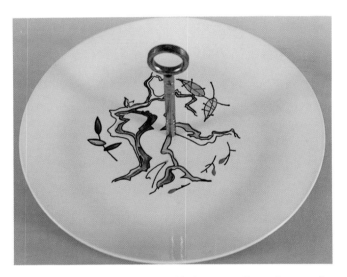

Skyline shape, center-handled server, "Windy Day."

Skyline shape, "Tanglewood."

Skyline shape, "Friendship" (left); "Sandy" (right).

Skyline shape, "Brown Daisy."

Skyline shape, "Stitches."

Skyline shape, "Mississippi."

Skyline shape, "Southern Starburst."

Skyline shape, "Barber Pole Palm."

Skyline shape, "Spokes."

Skyline shape, "Cherry Time." This is one of the Talisman Wallpaper patterns.

Skyline shape, "Vegetable Patch" platter.

Skyline shape, "Sweet Strawberries."

Skyline shape, "Carly's Apple."

Skyline shape, "Vegetable Soup." Also found on Candlewick.

Skyline shape, "Tartan Fruit."

Skyline shape, "Waldorf Salad."

Skyline shape, "Homestead."

Skyline shape: "Street's Barnyard" (left); "Flower Fantasy" (right).

Skyline shape, "Flower Barrels."

Skyline shape, "Tranquility" platter.

Skyline shape, "Three Sisters."

Skyline shape, "Annette."

Skyline shape: "Trinket" (left), large plate has three sprigs; "Cakewalk" (right).

Skyline shape, "Pyracantha."

Skyline shape, "Andante."

Skyline shape, "Scarlet Lily."

Skyline shape, "Charlotte."

Skyline shape, "Athens."

Skyline shape, "Bedecked."

Skyline shape, "Glimmer." This is another of the Designer Series.

Skyline shape, "Soubrette." Another Designer Series plate.

Skyline shape, "Alma's Fruit Salad." Notice this plate is signed "Alma, '55" on the front. Evidently made by one of the painters for herself.

Skyline shape, "Chicken Feed."

Skyline shape, "Hen, 1a" marked on back.

Skyline shape, "Pa, #1" marked on back.

Skyline shape, "Willa."

Square shape, "Flashy." This one has the PV in a circle mark.

Square shape, "Green Grape." These square plates were often painted on special order, or to go with another dinnerware pattern.

Square shape, "Tulip Treat."

Square shape, "Josey's Posies."

Square shape, "Susie Q."

Square shape, "Cornflower."

Square shape, "Spring Willow."

The following half-dozen squared or rounded square plates came from the collection of Albert Price, S.P.'s sales manager. We understand they were never put into production. Pictured above are "Zinnia" (left); "Festoon" (right).

Rounded square, "Fiddlesticks" (left); "Deja Vu" (right).

Rounded square, "Brilliance" (left); "First Love" (right).

Square shape, "Carousel."

Handled cake plate with fine ribbing, "Laurel Wreath."

Lace Edge shape, "Goldmont."

Waffle Edge, "Holly Wreath."

Heavy platter, "Leaf & Bar."

A CLOSER LOOK

One day when Bill was taking edge photographs for the Shapes section of this book, I thought, "Aren't those close-up patterns gorgeous!" So, we decided to do a few more "just for pretty." We hope you enjoy them and we also hope you will try this kind of photography with your own cameras. And most important of all — be sure to look closely!

This beauty got us started taking "a closer look." Unfortunately, it was done so long ago that the name of the pattern has escaped us!

"Falling Leaves."

"Country Garden."

"Wildwood Flower."

"White Mill." Notice the water pouring off the bottom of the wheel, and the various colors in the trees.

Artist-signed Quail Plate.
Did you ever notice that the quail is after some sort of many-legged bug?

Sample plate in the "Chicken Pickins" pattern.

Indian Character Jug.
I've had this for years and the necklace and the colorful rings around the hair just never particularly registered.

Indian Character Jug. What a lot of work in all those feathers!

Pioneer Woman Character Jug. This shows the ruffle at the bottom of the bonnet.

THE PROVINCIAL LINE

Most Blue Ridge collectors are well acquainted with the "French Peasant" pattern, which has become the most sought-after and most expensive pattern in the dinnerware line. It seems that during World War II, large stores that usually imported Quimper Pottery (pronounced *Kom-pair*) from France found markets cut off and asked Southern to design a pattern that was similar. Thus, the birth of the "French Peasant" pattern which can be found on china pieces as well as earthenware or semi-porcelain.

Quimper, of course, is a French pottery — very old — dating from the 1600s. In the 1860s, they began producing their Breton Peasant pattern, and it is obvious in comparing the two, that Southern Potteries' designers just sat down and copied the pattern for their own Provincial line. The border flowers are somewhat different shapes on the Southern Potteries' version, but the colors and the central motif are pretty much the same. The little evergreen tree standing to the left of the figure is simplified in the Southern Potteries' design, being only a vertical line with straight horizontal lines through it. The Quimper version is more realistic. All the Quimper I've ever seen has been marked as such, so there's no confusion of sources. French pottery is still being produced today, including the Breton Peasant pattern. We show some of the Quimper ware in photos included in this section.

In the early 1940s, Southern Potteries began producing "French Peasant" for all its customers. It was such a success that they decided to add more patterns with the French Provincial feeling, gradually introducing "Normandy," "Picardy," "Calais," "Brittany," "Lyonnaise," and "Orleans" along with the Provincial Farm Scene series.

In the Provincial Line, some pieces feature only a woman or a man, while larger pieces feature the couple. Various shapes of hollow ware, vases, teapots, pitchers, etc., will have the man on one side and the woman on the other. A pair of shakers will have the man on one shaker and the woman on the other.

Edge colors on "French Peasant" will vary with some having blue and rose-red and some, blue and rust. Which color treatment came first is still a mystery. Perhaps this took place when the exclusive contracts with large department stores ran out and "French Peasant" was made for everyone. Today, collectors pay premium prices for any of the Provincial Line. Be careful when buying, as Knowles Pottery also has a very similar Provincial type pattern that will fool you from a distance. Luckily, they marked all their wares.

On Skyline, the lady in the "Normandy" pattern.

Left: Lovely bowl in "Le Coq Soleil" pattern, Candlewick shape. Right: Plate in "Le Coq" pattern.

The Lady and the Gentleman plates in the "Lyonnaise" pattern.

Range shakers also in "Lyonnaise."

Demi cup and saucer in "Brittany" pattern on Clinchfield shape. There are two men and two ladies in each set.

"Calais," Astor shape (left). "Picardy," Clinchfield shape (right).

Two plates from the Provincial Farm Scenes series. These have been found on several different shapes, plus the little 6" square plates. "Mowing Hay" on Candlewick (left). "Watering the Flowers" on Skyline (right).

"Orleans," Colonial shape. This is one of the more elusive Provincial patterns.

"French Peasant" oval demi tray, with the lady only.

"French Peasant" covered vegetable on Colonial shape.

12" "French Peasant" platter on Colonial shape.

Two views of the "French Peasant" covered toast. Notice that the lady is on the lid (left) and the gentleman on the underplate (right).

This is a variation of the "French Peasant" pattern that we are calling "French a la Mode." Note the different edge with the original "French Peasant" having two rose-red flowers at the end of the leaf spray, and four blue dots forming a square between sprays. "French a la Mode" has alternating rusty-red and blue flowers in a continuous wreath around the edge, and no dots.

A lovely setting of "Lyonnaise" pattern. See all the pieces you can find?

A number of pieces are available in the "Calais" pattern, and this photo does not show them all!

A lovely demi pot, demi cups and demi saucers in "Brittany."

The original "Quimper" pattern from which "French Peasant" was taken. These dresser boxes were sent to me from France during World War II. Notice that the pattern is in shades of blue.

The Quimper mark on the set of dresser boxes.

Another Provincial "look-alike," this one made by Knowles China Company, not Southern Potteries.

CHILDREN'S AND INFANT SETS

There were two major types of children's ware produced by Southern Potteries. First, there is the Child's Set or Child's Tea Set. We have seen one of these in the original brown cardboard box with "Child's Set" stenciled on it. This consists of the demi pot, demi sugar and creamer, and four demi cups and saucers, plus four 6" plates. These sets are really darling, and if you can get one, it will certainly do wonders for your collection.

The second children's set is the Infant or Toddler Feeding Set. This set usually consisted of a cereal bowl, plate, and mug or these three pieces with the addition of a deep, heavier feeding dish. Divided dishes will also be found, along with a number of child-style decorated plates. All these came in many different patterns. Southern Potteries made enough child-friendly pieces to form a great collection on their own.

Skyline shape, "Burro" pattern. We understand a couple of decorators did three of these during their lunch hour.

Divided baby feeding dish in the "Baby's Pets" pattern. As you can see, this was made for a very special little boy.

Cereal bowl, plate, and mug in the "Baby's Pets" pattern: "Mother Goose" (left), "Blue Lamb" (center), "Piggy Blues" (right).

"Duck in Hat" child's plate on Piecrust blank.

"Baby's Squirrel" child's plate on Piecrust blank.

"Miss Mouse" child's plate on Piecrust blank.

"Lady Mouse" child's plate on Piecrust blank.

"Playful Puppy" child's plate on Piecrust blank.

The "Pink Puppy" set on Astor shape. The 7" plate has the puppy; the rest of the set consists of a 6⅜" cereal in "Blue Pig" and the 5 oz. "Yellow Rabbit" mug. The three-piece set sold in the Sears Roebuck 1943–1944 catalog for a whopping 95¢!

Cydney poses with her "Circus Elephant" cereal and "Performing Seal" mug.

A gathering of various children's pieces.

Top row: "Blue Pig" cereal (left), part of the "Pink Puppy" set. "Mama Goose" (right) from the "Pig 'N Pals" set.

Bottom row: Mugs (left to right) are "Piggy Blues," "Sprout," "Lyonnaise," and "Bunny."

Close-up of children's mugs: "Sprout" (left) and "Piggy Blues" (right).

The two playful little piggies are from the *Three Little Pigs* movie by Disney. The movie came out in the 1930s and was received with great enthusiasm by people weary of the Depression.

Above: "Three Little Pigs" mug. This one has the Practical Little Pig that built the house too strong to be "huffed and puffed and blown down."

Below: The mark used on the bottom of the "Three Little Pigs" pieces.

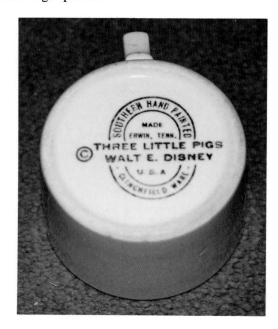

Top row: "Circus Elephant" cereal (left), "Clown" plate (right). Bottom row: "Jigsaw" feeding dish (left). "Mother Goose" cereal (right).

Plate, cereal, and mug in the "Bunny Hop" set on Skyline shape.

Cereal, plates, and mug in the "Fruit Children" set, Astor blank.

Pieces of the "Flower Children" set, Astor blank.

Cereal, plate, and mug in the "Humpty" pattern on Skyline shape.

Child's Tea Set in the "Painted Daisy" pattern, Colonial shape. This set consists of four each demi cups, demi saucers, and 6" plates; demi teapot, demi sugar and demi creamer.

HOLIDAY PATTERNS

Collectors jump for joy when they find the various lovely Blue Ridge holiday patterns. These include "Christmas Tree," "Christmas Tree with Mistletoe," "Poinsettia," and "Hollyberry," all on the Colonial blank, and "Christmas Doorway" on the Skyline shape. Of these, "Christmas Doorway" is the most elusive. It features a 10¼" dinner plate, a 6" round plate, cup, saucer, and Party Time Set consisting of a handled plate with cup well and matching cup.

For the Thanksgiving table, collectors hunt for "Thanksgiving Turkey" and "Turkey with Acorns." Mainly dinner plates, cups, saucers, and 15½" and 17½" platters have been found in these patterns. Plates are usually found on the Skyline blank while large platters will turn up on the Clinchfield blank. The luscious bowl of fruit on the "Still Life" pattern, Colonial shape, also makes a mouth-watering table, although plates are all that we have found to date.

Making your own holiday greeting cards using "tabletop" photos can be lots of fun. Some set-ups that we have used are shown in this section. (See Photographing Your Collection, p. 240 for more helpful hints).

Fanciful tabletop photo using "Thanksgiving Turkey" plate. Along with the plate are a Charlie Gibson apple paperweight and a Boyd's Crystal Art Glass covered turkey dish.

"Turkey with Acorns" platter on Skyline shape.

"Still Life" plate on Colonial shape.

"Christmas Tree" on Colonial shape.

"Christmas Tree with Mistletoe" on Colonial shape.

"Christmas Doorway" on Skyline shape. This design is more elusive than the other Christmas tree patterns.

"Christmas Doorway" in 10" and 6" plates, plus cup and saucer.

"Christmas Tree" party set in original box. Contains four party plates with cup well and four cups. Legends on box sides read: "For Patios and Parties" and "for Teatime and Television."

SALAD SETS

"Fruit Cocktail" salad set on Astor shape.

An overview of the "Language of Flowers" salad set on 8" Candlewick plates. These have the PV in a circle mark. Research has shown these were first made in France, marked "Porcelaine Opaque, MBCM, Monterfau, Made in France." See *Collector's Encyclopedia of Blue Ridge, Volume I* for closer view of the set, plus the translation of the mottos.

Fruited Plain Series, "Pineapple."

"Jubilee Fruit" set, on Colonial shape.

"Fruit Squares" salad set, 6" square plates, seven of the eight pieces are shown.

"Mexico Lindo" 5¾" square plates, five of the eight pieces are shown.

Top row: "Senoritas" (left), "Hat Dancer" (right).

Bottom row: "Mexican Woman" (left), "Peanut Vendor" (center), "Cock Fight" (right).

Most sets had eight plates. To date, we have also found the "Chicken Man" to this set, so we probably need two more.

Mandarin Series, 8" plates on Astor shape, "Chinese Junk" pattern.

Mandarin Series, "Blue Bottle Gourd."

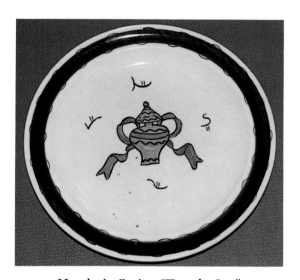

Mandarin Series, "Temple Jar."

Mandarin Series, "Pagodas."

Mandarin Series, "Pomegranate."

Mandarin Series, "Scroll."

Mandarin Series, "Plum Blossom."

Mandarin Series, "Shield."

Countryside Series, "Blackberry Vine."

Countryside Series, "Egg Basket."

Countryside Series, "Breezy Window." For more plates in this set, see *Collector's Encyclopedia of Blue Ridge Volume I* and *Southern Potteries Blue Ridge Dinnerware.*

Skyline Songbirds set, "Hooded Warbler."

Colonial Songbirds set, "Old Crow."

Astor Songbirds set, "Western Tanager." There are three Songbird sets — Skyline, Astor, and Colonial, each with eight different birds. For more illustrations, see *Collector's Encyclopedia of Blue Ridge, Volume I* and *Southern Potteries Blue Ridge Dinnerware.*

PITCHERS

BETSY BUSINESS

In the beginning, Betsy was earthenware rather than china (porcelain). She was sprayed or air brush painted. She is slightly smaller than the china version, a bit heavier, and seldom marked. The china or porcelain Betsys were introduced about 1945 and are almost invariably marked. You will also find Betsy made by The Cash Family, who marked their ware clearly with their name, so there should be no confusion. The small Betsy-like jugs often found at antiques malls and shows are imports and have nothing to do with Southern Potteries. We have on occasion found these marked "Made in Germany" and sometimes with a paper label marked "Made in Japan."

If you find a Betsy with a very white base color and all blue decoration including the blue dots on her cheeks, you probably have a new item sometimes found marked "Dedham Pottery."

Cherokee pottery also made some Betsys. The most notable difference we've seen is that her little shoes are often red, while Southern Potteries' Betsy has black shoes.

Left: Betsy Jug, "Melody" pattern. Right: Betsy Jug in earthenware decorated in blue. Notice label showing the contents of the jug to be Wrisley Bath Salts.

"Lavender Girl" Betsy, earthenware. Signed "M. Cook" on the bottom. Evidently, a Betsy painted by the decorator for herself.

China Betsy, "Daisies & Kisses" pattern.

"Polka Dot Chick" pitcher.

"Bloomingdale" pitcher, Palisades shape.

Palisades shape pitcher with unidentified pattern.

"Green Pear" pitcher, Palisades shape.

"Breakfast Bar" gravy boat on Candlewick. Also found on Skyline.

Grace shape pitcher in mottled earthenware.

Grace shape pitcher in mottled earthenware.

Martha shape jug with decorated scrollwork. Marked "Martha Jug, Dec. #1."

"Red Barn" pattern on Rebecca shape china pitcher.

"Sheree" pattern on Virginia shape pitcher (left), china, 4" mini. "Annette's Wild Rose" pattern on Antique shape pitcher (right), china, 3¼" mini.

"Anne" pattern, Antique shape (left), china, 4½" mini. "Orchard" pattern, Antique shape (right), china, 3¼" mini.

"Ginny" pattern on Grace Jug, china.

"French Peasant" on Helen shape pitcher.

"Lyonnaise" pitcher, Antique shape. Lady side (left), gentleman side (right).

"Opulence" pattern on Alice shape pitcher, china (left). "Nove Rose" pattern on Clara shape pitcher, china (center). "Eunice" pattern on Watauga shape pitcher, china (right).

Charm House Jug, china.

"Suwanee" pattern on Grace shape pitcher, china.

"Fall Colors" pattern on Antique shape pitcher.

"Rubeena" pattern on Antique mini pitcher, 4½", china.

Assortment of mini china pitchers (left to right): "Candied Fruit" pattern on 4" Antique shape, 4¼" Spiral shape, and 4½" Virginia; "Blue Iris" on 4½" Spiral shape; "Blue Peony" on 4½" Virginia shape.

More mini china pitchers (left to right): "Fall Colors" pattern on 4" Antique, 4¼" Virginia, and 4¼" Spiral; "Rubeena" on 4" Antique shape; "Melody" on 4" Antique shape; 4½" "Golden Age" on Virginia shape.

Antique shape, 6" pitcher.

Close-up views of the Mystery Transfer-Decorated pitchers described in *Collector's Encyclopedia of Blue Ridge, Volume I,* page 162. Advertised in a 1930 Butler Brothers catalog, these have the shape that says "Southern Potteries," but are not marked in any way. Nor does the advertisement mention maker, only that they are "American Semiporcelain Jugs." In handling the pitchers and comparing them with Blue Ridge, one can find no differences between them. These are all earthenware and transfer-decorated rather than china or porcelain and hand-painted. At this time, we still cannot *prove* manufacturer one way or the other.

4½" Antique shape pitcher (left); 4½" Watauga shape (right).

Two pitchers in Clara shape, 7" (left); 6⅝" (right).

Two more pitchers in Clara shape, 6¾" tall.

Two concave rib Abby shape pitchers, 5⅝" (left); 6¾" (right).

TEA, COFFEE & CHOCOLATE POTS

When is a teapot not a teapot? When it's a chocolate pot, of course! Or maybe a coffee pot. Confused? In the following pages you will find examples of the lovely pedestal china pot that we call a Chocolate Pot. One lucky day we found a number of these pieces in an old store stock, still in their original white gift boxes. Inside the pot was a printed slip of paper saying "This is Genuine Blue Ridge Hand-Painted Underglaze China. It is identified as a Chocolate Pot." The words "Chocolate Pot" were added with a stamp.

We wondered at the time why there was a matching sugar and creamer for a chocolate pot, and later asked a number of folks from Southern Potteries but nobody could shed any light on the matter. Awhile ago, some folks told us they had found chocolate pots that had "Teapot #1" marked on the bottom along with matching sugars and creamers with similar markings! Same pot — but now it's a teapot. To top all this off, the gentleman who was Southern Potteries' head mold maker told us that he remembered making the mold in the first place — from a silver coffee pot! When you think about it, china or silver coffee pots are usually tall and slim as opposed to the rounder, shorter teapot shapes.

The reasoning behind all these differences is simply this: Southern Potteries made whatever the customer wanted. If the customer wanted a chocolate pot — it was a chocolate pot; if they wanted a teapot with matching sugar and creamer — then it was a teapot. Remember, on the printed slip we found, the words "chocolate pot" were stamped. Workers could just as easily have stamped "teapot" or something else on other slips. This is not unusual. If the customer wanted a child's set, Southern used the demi pot and creamer and sugar, demi cups and saucer. If they wanted a breakfast set, the demi pot, and sugar and creamer were in that. If the dinnerware the customer wanted didn't normally come with a big pitcher or fancy relish or divided plate — the customer just told Southern what they wanted and they made one. Remember, they weren't producing dinnerware for collectors, they were producing it to sell and to use. The customer was always right!

Square Round shape in "Snowflake" pattern, marked "Coffee Pot" in gold on bottom.

Square Round shape in "Border Print" pattern.

Colonial shape in "Rose Marie" pattern, china.

Ovoid coffee pot in "Rose Marie" pattern.

Skyline shape in "Normandy" pattern.

Ball shape in "Lyonnaise" pattern.

Ball shape in "Song Sung Blue" pattern.

Skyline shape in "Green Apple" pattern.

Ball shape in "Sonora" pattern.

Ball shape in "Calais" pattern.

Woodcrest shape in black "Jungle Grass" pattern.

Skyline shape in "Peach Blossom" pattern.

Colonial shape in "Mickey" pattern (left); Mini Ball shape in "Gordon Violets" pattern (right).

Woodcrest shape in "Cock 'O the Morn" pattern.

Square Round shape in "Carol Ann" pattern.

Good Housekeeping marked pieces in "Candace" pattern.

Demi pot in "Brittany" pattern. Gentleman figure is on other side.

Demi pot, sugar, creamer, cup and saucer, "Snippet" pattern.

Demi pot and creamer in plain colored slip decoration.

Demi pot and creamer in "Wild Morning Glory" pattern.

Chocolate pot in "Red Barn" pattern.

Demi pot, sugar, creamer, and tray in "Yellow Nocturne" pattern.

Chocolate pot with pedestal sugar and creamer in "Swiss Dancers" pattern.

Chocolate pot in "Williamsburg Bouquet" pattern, both sides shown.

Chocolate pot, sugar, creamer, and demi cups and saucers in "Spring Bouquet" pattern.

China (porcelain) demi set in "Spring Bouquet" pattern.

Chocolate pot, sugar, creamer, and tray in "Midnight" pattern. Oddly enough, this is marked "Tea Set #2" on the bottom. Below shows the opposite side of the set.

Chocolate pot, sugar and creamer in "Romance" pattern.

Opposite side of "Romance" chocolate pot, sugar and creamer on tray.

Chocolate tray in "Romance" pattern. This set will be found with gray line trim and light green line trim.

TEA TILES

"Carolina Wren" 6" square tile.

"Rooster" 6" square tile.

"Bells" 6" square tile.

"Butterfly & Berry" 6" square tile.

"Cherry Fizz" 4" square tile.

"Minnesota Rose" 6" round tile.

"Pinkie Lee" 6" round tile.

"Rosmae" 6" round tile.

"Cowslip" 4" square tile.

"Quartet" 4" square tile.

"Fragrance" 6" square tile (left), "Carrie" 6" round tile (right).

"Summer Day" 6" square tile.

"Victory Garden" 6" square tile.

KITCHENWARE &
MISCELLANEOUS PIECES

Various pieces of the Waffle Set. "Leaf" syrup pitcher on Trellis shape (left), 5½" tall. The syrup is the elusive piece. Batter Jug on Colonial shape (right), "Tulip" pattern, 8" tall. Batter tray in "Red Bank" pattern, 13⅜" long.

Another view of the Batter Set in various colors of "Leaf" pattern.

Pie baker and lifter, "Josephine" pattern, Astor shape.

Heavy pie baker, "Burgundy" pattern.

Pie baker, "Cat's Paw" pattern.

Heavy pie baker, "Renegade" pattern.

Covered vegetable, "Dungannon" pattern.

Covered casserole in metal stand, "Triplet" pattern.

Covered casserole, "Happy Home" pattern.

Covered casserole, "Julie" pattern.

Three stacking leftovers in "Mountain Crab" pattern.

Two covered leftovers, "Kitchenette" pattern.

Three of four mixing bowls in set, "Leaf" pattern. Mixing bowls came in the following sizes: 9" x 4" high; 7½" x 3¾" high; 6⅞" x 3¼" high; 6" x 2⅞" high.

"Georgia" Lazy Susan set. This was shown in a 1951 N. Shure catalog for $11.50!

Three shallow baking dishes in "Leaf" pattern. Large dish is 10½" x 6¼". Small ones are 6½" x 5¼".

Three-tier tidbit, "Country Strawberry" pattern, wood center handle.

Three-tier tidbit in "Farley's Fruits" pattern, brass-plated center handle.

Butterdish with unnamed pattern. Maybe that hard-to-hold finial is the reason there are so few surviving today!

"Red Bank" two-spout gravy or sauce boat on attached tray. If this had not been marked, I would not have believed it!

Lifter in the "Berry Delicious" pattern.

10" heavy divided plate, marked "Mountain Glory, Blue Ridge Mountain Hand Art" on base.

Two china deviled egg plates. When these were made, we understand the process was timed and it was decided they could not be produced at a profit, so no more were made.

These are the bases of two deviled egg dishes. On the left, marked PV in a circle, is a Southern Potteries dish. The right piece is marked Ebling & Reuss with bell; this is not Southern Potteries. Notice the much larger round foot. Dishes also have been found with an "S" inside a plate mark, plus "Made in Germany" and "Made in France" marks. None of these, of course, are Southern Potteries.

SUGARS, CREAMERS & EGG CUPS

China demi sugar, "Magic Carpet" pattern.

Palisades shape covered sugar, "Pink Dogwood" pattern.

Demi creamer and sugar in "Fox Grape" pattern.

Squared handle sugar and creamer in a "Leaf" color variation.

The double egg cups originated in England where the smaller opening is used to set the whole egg in, while the larger opening is for the folks who like to take their egg out of the shell and mix it up with salt and pepper or whatever they like. "Irish Mary" pattern (left). "Irish Mary" will also be found in green and pink, rather than all green. "Sour Apples" pattern (right).

Creamer, possibly Trellis shape, unnamed pattern.

Covered sugar, Fifties shape, "Wild Cherry #1" pattern.

4¾" tall creamer carrying old Clinch-field mark, "Imogene" pattern.

"Dungannon" covered sugar, 5½" diameter.

SHAKERS

Pair of china shakers, unnamed pattern (left). Woodcrest shaker in "Tree" pattern (center). Blossom Top shakers (right).

Blossom Top shakers, "Granton's Rose" pattern.

Bud Top shakers with Good Housekeeping mark.

⇥ 145 ⇥

One of the colors of Hen and Rooster shakers. These also come in white with black accents, brown with multicolor patches, and a flashy multicolor allover pattern.

N O T I C E

The modern, accepted manner of sealing Salt and Pepper Shakers is with sanitary Scotch Tape. This Tape may be procured from any well stocked drug, stationery or department store for only a few cents, and comes in the handy home package. One piece of tape sufficient to seal a Shaker costs only a fraction of a cent and may be used for many fillings. This modern method of sealing permits the Shaker to set evenly upon any surface and replaces the old-fashioned method of corks, which will not permit the Shaker to rest evenly unless deeply depressed into the Shaker. And by so doing the cork is often pushed too far into the Shaker and thereby lost until it is extracted, piece by piece.

This "notice" was found packed in a box containing Blue Ridge shakers.

LAMPS

American Home lamp, "Indian Summer" pattern.

Fancy handled lamp, 10" tall, "Columbia" pattern.

American Home lamp, "Largo" pattern.

Lamp marked "Vanity Fair, Genuine Porcelain," (left). China is 10" tall; 21¾" overall with metal base, "Augusta" pattern.

Vanity Fair lamp (right), 18" overall, "Daisy Mae" pattern.

American Home lamp, "Leslie" pattern.

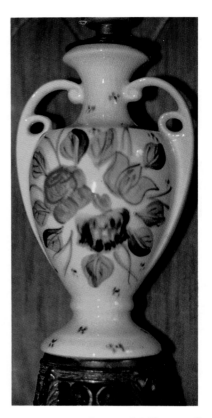

Vanity Fair lamp, "Gilbertine" pattern.

Pair of gold-decorated Betsy Jugs made into lamps.

VASES

Tapered 8" china vase, "Purple Crown" pattern.

Ruffle top vase in china, shows both sides of the "Elegance" pattern vase.

9¼" ruffle top vase (left), "French Peasant" pattern. Bud vase (right), "Fleurs" pattern, hard to find.

7¾" handled vase (left), "Fantasy" pattern. Bud vase (right), 5½" tall, "Greensleeves" pattern.

Ruffle top china vase (left), 9¼" tall, "Delphine" pattern. Bud vase (center), 5½" tall, hard to find. Boot vase (right), 8" tall, "Gladys" pattern. The 8" vase is the only boot vase that Southern Potteries made.

A selection of boot vases; only one was made by Southern Potteries.

Left to right: Made in Japan, 6" tall; Ebeling & Reuss, 7⅜" tall; Cash Family Clinchfield Artware, 8½" tall; Southern Potteries, 8" tall; Spaulding, 8¼" tall, decal trim and gold, larger than Southern boot.

BOWLS

Southern Potteries made a lot of bowls, from the beginning right through to the end. Following is a selection from all the eras — from the inception of hand painting until the pottery's closing.

"Lacey Muscat," Astor shape.

"Fruit Children" cereal bowl, Astor shape.

"Leaf" covered dish, color variation, Clinchfield shape.

Covered dish with lid, 9¼" diameter, "Ridge Ivy" pattern, Skyline shape.

Salad bowl and underplate, "Vegetable Soup" pattern, Candlewick shape.

Colonial shape, "Brownfield" pattern.

Vegetable bowl with wavy divider in center, "Red Bank" pattern.

Colonial shape , "Lemonade" pattern.

Piecrust shape, "Whipstitch" pattern.

6" Woodcrest shape, "Quilted Fruit" pattern.

Candlewick shape, "Berry Bowl" pattern.

Shirred egg dish, "Richmond" pattern. According to the old cookbooks, shirred eggs were baked in the oven with butter and bread or cracker crumbs which probably accounts for the browning on the bowl.

Skyline Studioware shape, "Grape Ivy" pattern.

Two hot cereal bowls, 4¾" diameter; 2¾" tall, "Crab Apple" pattern (left); "Soddy-Daisy" pattern (right).

Candlewick shape, "Petals" pattern.

Candlewick shape, "Annabell" pattern.

Candlewick shape, "Pretty Petals" pattern.

Palisades shape, 9" diameter, "Shimmer" pattern.

Candlewick shape, "Windwheel" pattern (left); Astor shape, "Valentine Asters" pattern (right).

Two Lace Edge bowls with different colored backgrounds, but the same hand-painted flowers. The pattern is called "Emma."

One of the older shape bowls with both hand painting and transfer decoration, "Spring Sisters" pattern.

Narrow Rib shape, "Confetti" pattern.

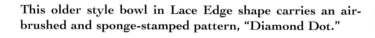

This older style bowl in Lace Edge shape carries an air-brushed and sponge-stamped pattern, "Diamond Dot."

Waffle Edge shape, "Midsummer Rose" pattern. This pattern will also be found on Colonial shape, as well as Curlicue Arches shape.

Two different patterns on Curlicue Arches shape; "Midsummer Rose" (left), "Melba Louise" (right).

Lace Edge shape, "Expo" pattern.

Lotus Leaf shape, "Red Willow" pattern.

Lotus Leaf shape, "Vicky" pattern.

Fish Scale shape, "Bunny Tails" pattern. Most background and edge colors on this shape are air-brushed.

Fish Scale shape, "Lacey Fans" pattern.

Two bowls on Fish Scale shape; "Garden Wedding" pattern (left), "Dreamy" pattern (right).

Fish Scale shape, "Dreamy" in another color.

Fish Scale shape, "Devilish" pattern.

Fish Scale shape, "Limelight" pattern.

Lace Edge shape, "Nightlight" pattern.

Candlewick shape, "Harlequin" pattern.

7" soup bowl in Lotus Leaf shape, "Spring Feathers" pattern.

Lotus Leaf bowl, "Jay" pattern.

Astor shape, "Autumn Splendor" pattern (left); Colonial shape, "Kent" pattern (right).

Waffle Edge shape, "Kelvin" pattern.

Basketweave edge shape, "True Blue" pattern.

Two Astor shape bowls. "Irene" pattern (left); color variation of "Nightlight" pattern (right).

Narrow Rib shape, "October Blue" pattern (left); Colonial shape, "Whip Tac" pattern (right).

Older Southern Potteries/Clinchfield marking on bowl, "Sweet William" pattern.

Lace Edge bowl, "Michelle" pattern.

Two Lace Edge shape bowls, "Sprite" pattern (left); "Belle" pattern (right).

Curlicue Arches shape, "Abigail" pattern. Notice the very Art Deco stamp trim.

Astor shape, "Callie" pattern.

Two Skyline shape bowls. "Friendship Plaid" (left), this one has an edge that looks like it needs a lid; "Beatrice" pattern (right).

Narrow Rib shape, "Glenda" pattern (left); Squared Rib shape, "Daisy Chain" pattern (right).

Candlewick shape, "Kelly" pattern.

"French Knots" pattern on covered casserole-type dish.

Two covered dishes. "Rock Rose" pattern (left), 8¼" diameter, 3" deep, carries "Oven Proof" mark; "Prim" pattern (right), 8" diameter, 3¾" deep.

Lace Edge shape, "Triangle" pattern (left); Scroll Edge shape, "Mud Pie'" pattern (right).

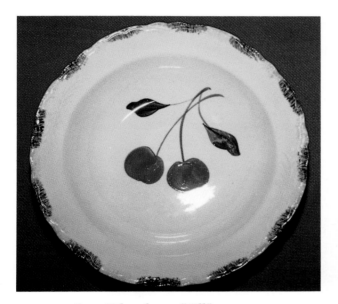

Lace Edge shape, "Jill" pattern.

Colonial shape, "Singleton" pattern.

Stick-handled ramekin in "Elegance" pattern.

Covered dish in "Albert" pattern, 8½" diameter.

Palisades shape, "Gray Day" pattern.

TRAYS & RELISHES

Celery tray, Skyline shape, "Orchid" pattern.

Celery, china, Leaf shape, "Melody" pattern.

Celery, china, Leaf shape, "Red Barn" pattern.

Celery, china, Leaf shape, "Blue Scatter" pattern.

Mod Leaf shape, "Rose Garden" pattern, china (left); celery, china, Leaf shape "Fruit Basket" pattern, (right).

Flat shell bon-bon tray, china, Dorothy shape, "Fruit Basket" pattern.

Flat shell, china, "Pixie" pattern (left); Maple Leaf cake tray, china, "Verna" pattern (right).

Flat shell, "Fox Grape" pattern. We do not find many china pieces in this pattern, but this is one.

Cake tray, china, Maple Leaf shape, "Millie's Pride" pattern.

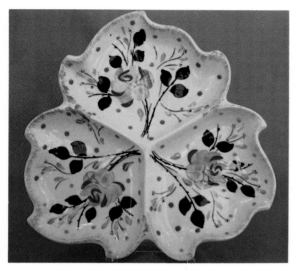

Snack tray, china, Martha shape, "Roses & Dots" pattern.

Snack tray, china, Martha shape, "Palace" pattern.

Demi tray plus open Colonial sugar and creamer, all in "Nocturne" pattern.

Cup, saucer (regular size), and demi tray, all in "Ashley's Bouquet" pattern on Colonial shape.

Two demi trays in "French Peasant" pattern. Colonial shape (left); Skyline shape (right).

China demi tray, Colonial shape, "Summersweet" pattern.

Four-section divided relish, china, "Raining Violets" pattern.

Two deep shell relishes in china, "Mayflower Bouquet" (left), stamped on back "Shell Bon-Bon #1"; "Rose of Sharon" pattern (right).

Chocolate tray, china, "Rose of Sharon" pattern.

Four individual relishes in "Veggie #2" pattern.

Charm House divided relish tray, china.

Waffle tray, "Daisy Chain."

"Anniversary Song" tray.

BOXES

Individual ashtray, "Naughty" pattern (left); square cigarette box, "Sheree" pattern, 4½" size (right).

Square cigarette box and one ashtray, "Sunset Sails" pattern. Sets came with four ashtrays in the box.

Square cigarette box with two ashtrays, "Dusty" pattern.

Round candy box in "Heather Bouquet" pattern. This one has decal decoration and gold trim so was probably an early one.

Sherman Lily box, china, "American Beauty" pattern.

"Rose Step" box, china (left); "Seaside" box, china (right).

"Lyonnaise" pattern cigarette box and ashtrays.

ASHTRAYS

Confederate Monument round ashtray, 5" diameter. On the back is "First State Bank, Erwin, Tennessee" in gold.

This is the ashtray shape that fits with the Mallard box. In earthenware, this pattern is "120 Volts." Probably made by a worker for their own personal use.

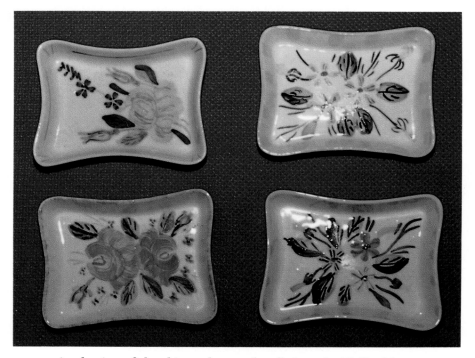

A selection of the china ashtrays that fit into the Mallard box.

Two of the "eared" ashtrays. On the back of the right-hand tray is "Compliments of the People's Bank, Johnson City, Tenn."

5" round ashtray, "Nove Rose" pattern, signed "Alleene Miller" on the back.

5" round ashtray, "Show Off" pattern. On the back is "Compliments of the People's Bank, Johnson City, Tenn."

5" round ashtray with a violet pattern.

5" round ashtray, "Border Print" pattern.

5" round ashtray, "Contrary Mary" pattern. On the back is the legend: "Southern Potteries Inc., Warranted Gold 22K, Made in U.S.A.," all in gold.

FIGURINES

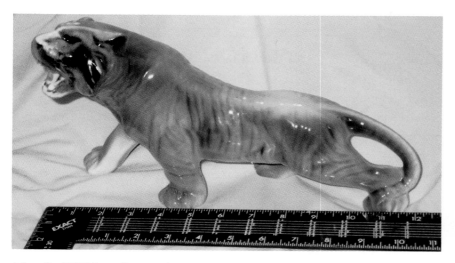

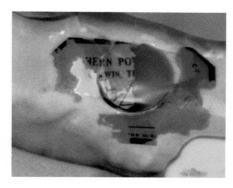

A lovely 12½" long lioness figurine, with, thankfully, a Southern Potteries sticker on her tummy. We have mentioned a number of times that unless an animal or other figurine is marked "Southern Potteries" or has what seems to be an original label, there is no way to authenticate the manufacturer. In the book *Morton Potteries – 99 Years* by Doris & Burdell Hall, this same lioness is shown on page 107 as a product of the Cliftwood Art Potteries in Morton, Illinois. A fine example of the way in which various potteries "borrowed" molds from each other.

These two nude figure flower holders are marked "Southern Potteries, Inc." on the bottom of the piece.

THE SAME ONLY DIFFERENT
PATTERN VARIATIONS

"It's the same, but not quite the same" is something we've been bewailing ever since we began the sorting process for these Blue Ridge books. You may find the same patterns done in different colors such as "Leaf," "Wild Cherry," "Spiderweb," "Moss Rose," "Southern Rose," "Whirligig," etc. Or you'll find a pattern on various blanks where the central motif is the same, but the decorative edge treatments are different, such as "Hawaiian Fruits."

In the "Nocturne" pattern, the flowers are red; in "Yellow Nocturne" they are yellow, but with the same design and placement. In "Bluefield," the flowers are blue with rose and black leaves. Another pattern has surfaced with the same flowers, buds, and leaf placement, but the flowers and buds are yellow and the leaves brown! "Irish Mary" will be found with all green flowers and leaves and also in shades or rose and pink. "Mardi Gras" will be found on Candlewick and Colonial blanks, some with red edge treatments, some with black line edge trim and some with a plain edge. Placement of buds and leaves also will vary, as shown in the photograph in this chapter. "Moss Rose" will be found with chartreuse and gray flowers and also with brown and pink flowers.

"Daisy Chain" cups and saucers have been found on a square shape and also on Trellis shape. Cups with square handles have the "chain" painted inside the cup. On the Trellis cup, the "chain" is on the outside.

In fruit patterns, placement of the various fruits will sometimes be different, which causes no end of difficulties (including crossed eyes and headaches). Personally, small differences in patterns don't bother me — we love the artistic variations and misplaced motifs. After all, it is hand-painted!

The "Leaf" or "Antique Leaf" pattern will be found in the following colors: yellow, blue, red; black, yellow, red; green, yellow, red; black, red, dark green, and, in the case of "Red Leaf," all red.

"Wild Cherry" pattern will be found in the following color variations: #1, brown/white with yellow berries; #2, pink/gray with white berries; #3, brown/gold with red berries; #4, aqua/gray with white berries.

"Spiderweb" will be found with little gray or charcoal "webs" on the following background colors: pink, blue, mint green, yellow, white, and peach — at least, that's what has surfaced so far.

In this assortment of pieces in Peggie's Posies pattern, one can plainly see how the smaller pieces differ in pattern content from the larger pieces, causing no end of confusion.

An assortment of "Chablis" pattern pieces.

Another example in "Tiny" pattern on Trailways shape.

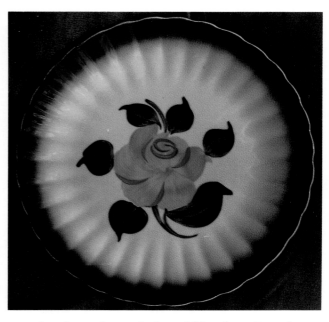

Color variation of "Southern Rose" pattern.

Another color variation of "Southern Rose."

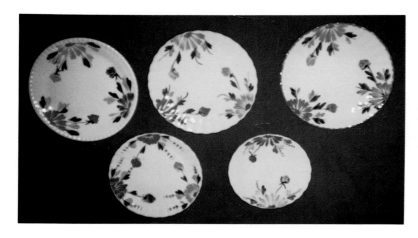

This photo illustrates the various differences found in the "Mardi Gras" pattern. Some of the pieces are on Candlewick shape, some on Colonial. Some Candlewick pieces are marked "Mt. Vernon" on the back.

Two versions of the "Moss Rose" pattern. Different colors and even different leaf placement.

Two views of "Daisy Chain" cup and saucer with different leaf placements, etc.

"Whirligig" pattern, Colonial shape (left); "Bow-Knot" pattern, Piecrust shape (right). Same flowers, different colors, slightly different leaves.

Covered sugar bowl in Fifties shape, "Wild Cherry #1" pattern (left). Plate in the "Wild Cherry #4" pattern (right). In this stamp-and-fill-in pattern, we have four variations: #1 is reddish-brown with white and gold berries; #2 is pink with gray and white berries; #3 is brown and gold with white berries; #4 is aqua and gray with white berries.

In the "Leaf" or "Antique Leaf" pattern, there are many color variations. This is the green-yellow-red version.

"Antique Leaf" or "Leaf" in all red and in yellow-blue-red.

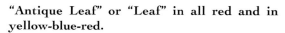

"Antique Leaf" or "Leaf" in yellow-blue-red and in black-yellow-red.

"Leaf" mixing bowl in yellow-black-red.

Maybe we should call this "Oops!" Decorators told us that sometimes when they made a mistake in their pattern, they just washed off the mistake. In this stamp-on case, the good piece is on the Candlewick shape, but it seems when they washed off a mistake on the Colonial shape, the leaves from the "mistake" pattern still show!

ADVERTISING PIECES

Southern Potteries did quite a big business producing advertising pieces such as ashtrays, bowls, plates, and pitchers for various business places and individuals. These little items add lots of interest to a collection. Southern also produced the large, palette-shaped advertising plates both for themselves and for Primrose China and Talisman Wallpaper. Lucky is the collector who can boast having all three!

Three pieces from the Talisman Wallpaper selection. The Colonial shape on the left is "Yorktown." Center cup is "Blossom Tree." Right is "Cherry Time." In 1950–1952, United Wallpaper Co. had the idea to produce several coordinated wallpaper and chinaware patterns. The idea did not prove successful and was abandoned after a short period.

5½" round ashtray picturing the Confederate Monument located in Stone Mountain, Georgia. Advertising for the First State Bank in Erwin, Tennessee, on front.

This "Stanhome Ivy" patterned piece embellished with the Eastern Star says "from Marie Mutchmore, Lincoln, Neb." in gold.

5" round ashtray advertises the ET & WNC Transportation Company, serving North Carolina, South Carolina, Tennessee, Virginia with "Dependable Freight Service."

People's Bank advertisement on the back of 5½" round ashtray.

5½" round ashtrays advertising Clinchfield Railroad Co.

Bowl, Watauga shape, "Fabulous" pattern. Wording is "Compliments of Ritter Furn. Co., Nashville, Tenn."

Candlewick shape plate, "Janice" pattern, printed in gold on the front is: "Xmas Greetings, Patsy Warner, Richlands, Va."

Grace shape pitcher in earthenware. On the squiggly decoration are the words: "Merry Xmas and Happy New Year, C.C. Long, Trammell, Va."

8" fish plate with Lace Edge shape, Clinchfield era. Logo is: "Compliments of T. A. Watson, Medville, Kans."

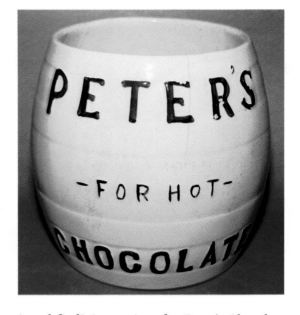

A real find! A container for Peter's Chocolate which is 8¼" tall and about the same in diameter. Must have been either for a little coffee shop operation or a premium for the home. We think it should have a lid, but none was found with it.

Small shallow bowl-shaped piece commemorating Southern Potteries Employees Fourth Annual Outing, Labor Day, 1920.

Blue Ridge counter sign in "Colonial Bouquet" pattern.

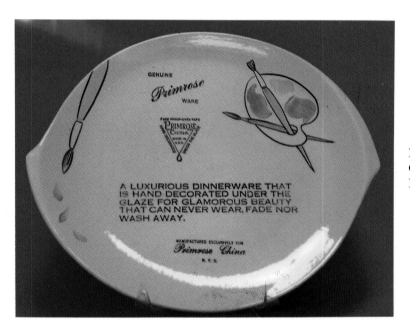

Large advertising plate for the Primrose China Company which was a jobber for Southern Potteries.

Large advertising plate for Blue Ridge dinnerware.

GLASSWARE

In the mid 1940s, Earl Newton, a sales representative for Southern Potteries, started a small glass factory in Bowling Green, Ohio. His decorators learned patterns and techniques from Southern's decorators, and Newton began producing glassware decorated to match Southern's patterns. Later, Newton augmented his supply of glass with various shapes and sizes of blanks from Libby Glass and Federal Glass, decorating on both frosted and clear backgrounds.

Decorating glassware can be a very different task compared to decorating chinaware. Ceramic type colors were necessary for permanence, but these required the glassware to be subjected to heat enough to fuse the colors permanently. A number of problems arose in developing the ceramic colors since those used often appeared different after firing. Red might fire to pink; orange to light peach. Pastels became brilliant when fused.

Since glass is more in danger of cracking upon rapid changes in temperature, a lehr had to be used in which the glass entered at room temperature, was gradually brought up to a firing temperature of about 1,200°, and then slowly cooled again to room temperature. Using this method caused what is called a re-annealing which made the glass even stronger than the original. The artists were then given a training period after which they copied the original master design, much the same as was done in the pottery.

In December of 1991, an article written by Donna McGrady on Gay Fad Studios appeared in *Antique Week* publication. So many things in this excellent article lead us to believe that some of the "Blue Ridge" glassware we're finding may well have been decorated by Gay Fad. This company was located in Lancaster, Ohio, and operated from 1943 to 1963. They did not make glass, but purchased blanks from Hazel Atlas (H over A mark), Federal Glass (F inside a shield mark), Libby Glass (script L mark), and West Virginia Specialty Company. Some Gay Fad products will have an interlocked GF somewhere on the glass. They decorated with both silk screen method and hand painting, on frosted or clear backgrounds. They also decorated on milk glass and on clear glass painted white inside and decorated on the outside. Many pieces have gold or silver trim.

According to McGrady's article, Gay Fad decorated glassware to go with Royal China Company patterns, Metlox Poppy Trail patterns, and Stetson's Dixie Dogwood, to name just a few. Plaid sets to compliment Vernon Kilns Plaids or Blair's Gay Plaid dinnerware are also mentioned in the article. You may recall that Southern Potteries produced some dinnerware for Blair also. Considering that Gay Fad decorated matching glasses for Stetson, it only stands to reason that they probably did go-withs for Blue Ridge patterns also, although we have no solid paperwork proof of this.

Be careful when you buy — it really makes no difference who decorated the items, just as long as they really do match your pattern. Keep in mind that if a couple of companies were doing this, there should be a lot of glassware to be found, and paying high prices is a no-no. One last word or warning — *do not* put these decorated glasses through the dishwasher. I have learned, in buying and selling decorated souvenir and promotional glassware, that patterns dulled by the dishwasher have little or no value to collectors.

Catalogs have been found to verify that several pottery patterns had matching glassware, such as 11 oz. tumblers, 6 oz. juice, and 7½ oz. dessert cups.

So far, we have found these three items of matching glassware for the following patterns: "Bamboo," "Country Fruit," "Red Barn," "Crab Apple," "Cumberland," "Green Briar," "Mountain Ivy," "Petal Point," "Ridge Daisy," "Ridge Harvest," "Ridge Ivy," "Sun Bouquet," "Vibrant," "Whirligig," "Dahlia," "Red Rooster," "Susan," "Chintz," "Poinsettia" (frosted), "Baltic Ivy," "County Fair," "Damascus," and "Mountain Cherries." Probably there are more out there.

Norma Lilly, publisher of the *Blue Ridge Newsletter,* researched and found Montgomery Ward's 1953 spring and mid-summer sales books show "Green Briar," "Sun Bouquet," and "Baltic Ivy" with no glassware; Ward's 1954–55 fall and winter catalog lists "Baltic Ivy," "Crab Apple," "Country Fruit," and "Bamboo" with only the 11 oz. tumblers; advertisements in a 1955 gift catalog (not identified) show "Red Rooster," "Whirligig," "Damascus," and "Mountain Cherries" with tumblers only.

Matching glassware on frosted background: "Sunfire" (left); "Strawberry Sundae" (center); "Fruit Fantasy" (right).

More matching glassware: "Tick-Tack" (left); "Bluebell Bouquet" (center); "Poinsettia" (right).

TABLE SETTINGS

Look what other collectors have done with their Blue Ridge. Colored glassware or crystal — either one is beautiful!

"Christmas Tree with Mistletoe" holiday table.

"Magnolia" Blue Ridge with amber goblets makes a lovely setting.

Amethyst tumblers give "Peony" pattern a lift.

Marigold carnival glassware with "Orange Tulip" Blue Ridge makes an eye-catching display cabinet.

"Full Bloom" with complimentary Bohemian amethyst cut-to-crystal tumblers. Rose-pink napkins pick up the color of the second bloom.

THE MANY FACETS OF BLUE RIDGE

We have found over the years that Blue Ridge collectors are endlessly inventive when it comes to finding unique ways to enjoy their collections, everything from very personal greeting cards and stationery to Blue Ridge-decorated Christmas trees and special occasion cakes. Artist Lee Frye Burrow sometimes visits shows with her Blue Ridge paintings, two of which we share here. Tabletop photos are a lot of fun to put together and make great notecards or holiday cards. Read "Photographing Your Collection," p. 240, for some tips.

Christmas tree decorated with Blue Ridge plates. Crocheted snowflakes give a wintry feeling to this great tree.

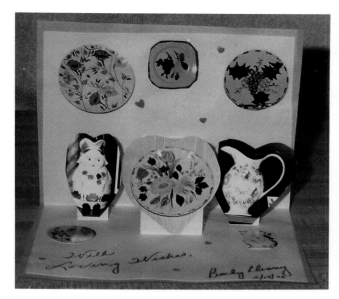

Blue Ridge photos were cut up to make this innovative Valentine.

Even birthday cakes can be decorated to match the birthday girl's favorite patterns.

Artist Lee Frye Burrow visits the Blue Ridge show with her paintings. I couldn't resist this one!

These lovely Christmas ornaments were purchased this year by a collector, signed "Suzanne '96."

Another Lee Frye Burrow painting. Since I'm a "cat person" as well as a Blue Ridge collector, you know this one ended up on my wall also.

TABLETOP PHOTOS

Doing "tabletop" photos is a great hobby. These photos also make wonderful greeting cards or notepaper.

"Wild Turkey" platter along with the Indian Character Jug. Add some Indian corn and a few autumn leaves and you're all set.

"Cock 'O the Morn" platter with various patterns of chicken shakers. I think they're waking the farmer up so he can get started with his plowing.

The "Circus Elephant" bowl and "Performing Seal" mug are all set for the day's show. Flanking them are two Fenton Art Glass Co. clown figures.

The "Windmill" plate makes a good background for our hen and rooster shakers. They're ready to pick up the corn evidently dropped from the old International's wagon.

A calm scene with the "White Mill" as background for the Mallard shakers.

SOUTHERN'S PAPER GOODS

Collecting Blue Ridge can be more than just collecting dishes. There are many collectors with beautiful albums of old advertising, for instance. Most advertisements were black and white, but you will find some in lovely color. Put them in a three-ring binder in clear plastic pages. Be sure to put a little sticker on the plastic page (not on the ad), giving the magazine or catalog name and the date. Ads can be found in magazines like *House Beautiful, Better Homes & Gardens, American Home,* etc.; also in Sears Roebuck, Montgomery Ward, Spiegel, and Butler Brothers catalogs of the period.

Another fun thing is looking through the pages of magazines such as women's *Ladies' Home Journal, Woman's Home Companion,* etc. Hunt for illustrated food articles that often used Blue Ridge in their table settings. Various ads are often found for other products displayed on Blue Ridge pieces. Home style magazines often featured Blue Ridge in the cabinets, cupboards and shelves of the homes illustrated. Look for Blue Ridge in and on furniture advertised in the big mail-order catalogs as well. Small, pamphlet-type cookbooks of the era are another fertile field for this type of illustration. All these items make fascinating albums that not only illustrate Blue Ridge, but also can trace the changes in our way of life over the years.

If you're lucky, you may run across old Southern Potteries stock certificates, insurance company certificates or Southern Potteries letterheads such as those shown in this section. Old photographs of parades and workers' get-togethers can sometimes be found also. The union booklets detailing the employees' working conditions of the era make fascinating reading. Original brochure pages from Southern Potteries are a great find. Keep in mind that Southern did not issue catalogs, just the occasional single brochure-type page.

Original Southern Potteries gift or packing boxes (with or without chinaware) also make good additions to a paper collection. Cardboard packing boxes often mention the contents such as "20-piece set" or "Child's Play Set" while store-display boxes may have contained Christmas snack sets or special order items ordered by various stores and given away "with purchase." The Mother's Oats boxes advertising Southern Potteries sets you could send away for are another great addition to your collection. Especially lucky is the collector who finds a Talisman Wallpaper sample book containing the papers made to go with Southern Potteries' dishes.

Hard to find but great to have are advertising banners or posters. And a real wonder for any paper collection is the album, a few pages of which are shown here. We're not certain what the album was for, or who lovingly assembled it, but lucky is the collector who owns it. (Not me, darn it!)

This Southern Belle box originally contained Blue Ridge dinnerware used as a premium in grocery stores.

"Flower Children" Child's Set packed originally in this Blue Ridge box. Here we have the 6⅞" deep feeding dish, 6½" cereal bowl, 8¼" plate, and 2⅝" tall mug.

Another gift box, this time enclosing the "Poinsettia" demi pot.

This Blue Ridge gift box contained a "Melody" pattern relish tray. Notice the little enclosure calling this a #1000 relish. The gold sticker on the box tells us that it was purchased at H. I. Smith, Stationery & Gifts, Phoenerville, Pa.

Identified as the Leaf Cake Plate, this "Millie's Pride" piece is also enclosed in a Blue Ridge gift box.

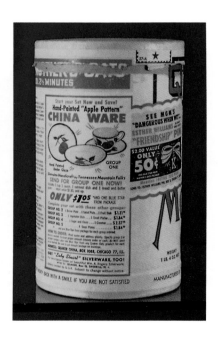

In 1953, Quaker Oats offered a four-piece set consisting of a cup, saucer, cereal bowl, and plate decorated with a single red apple and three green leaves on the Candlewick blank. Pictured is a set with its original mailing box. On the right is the Quaker Oats box that advertised the Blue Ridge premium.

Not as pretty as the gift boxes, but interesting all the same is this original packing box containing a 20-piece set of "Wild Rose."

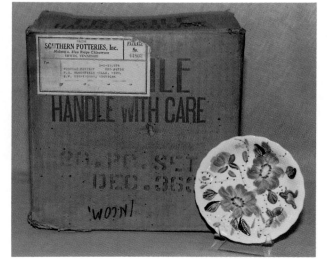

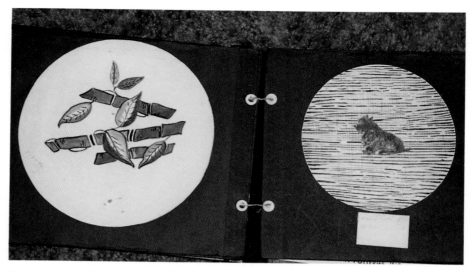

One lucky collector found this album of hand-drawn and colored Blue Ridge patterns. Who the original artist was, is a mystery.

Old photographs are a great find for the collector. This is a view of Southern Potteries in 1950.

Fifty shares of common stock issued to John A. Black on January 27, 1948.

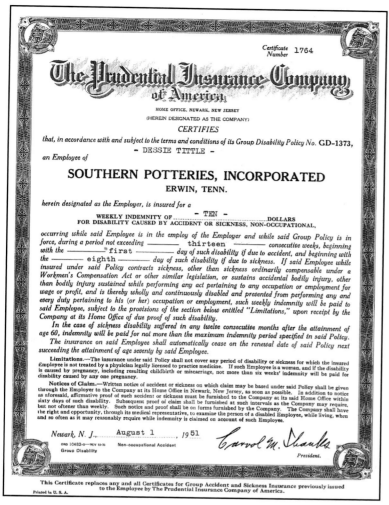

The Prudential Insurance Company's group disability policy for Southern Potteries, Inc. It was issued to Dessie Tittle on August 1, 1951.

White, Granite and Semi-Porcelain

WAGE SCALE and SIZE LIST AGREEMENT

BETWEEN

The National Brotherhood of Operative Potters

AND

The United States Potters Association

FEBRUARY, 1942

Cover of *White, Granite and Semi-Porcelain Wage Scale and Size List Agreement* between *The National Brotherhood of Operative Potters* and *The United States Potters Association,* February, 1942. See excerpts on pages 238 and 239.

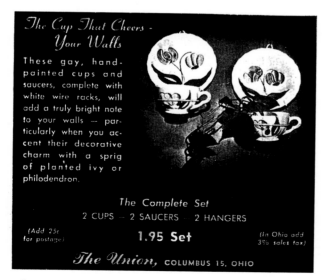

Advertisement for Blue Ridge cup and saucer set with wire racks.

Advertisement for "Cup • N • Plate" wall lamp.

B L U E   R I D G E
D I N N E R W A R E

Style blends with Beauty

— IN NEW *Skyline* dinnerware

Blue Ridge Ware captures a rainbow range of color harmonies to please the most particular taste. Today's styling demands color-bright charm and Blue Ridge offers a gay array of Skyline patterns for a fashion-wise choice.

The distinctive personality of genuine Hand Painted patterns plus the durability of Underglaze decorations and its modest cost make Blue Ridge an outstanding dinnerware value.

NATIONALLY ADVERTISED IN FOUR LEADING HOME MAGAZINES

SOUTHERN POTTERIES, INC.
ERWIN, TENNESSEE

REPRESENTATIVES

Cox & Company 208 Fifth Avenue New York 10, N. Y.	Earl W. Newton & Associates 1563 Merchandise Mart Chicago 54, Ill.	United Potteries Company Renkert Building Canton 2, Ohio	United China & Glass Company 400-420 Canal Street New Orleans 6, La.
David A. Page 2104 Wayland Street Charlotte, N. C.	D. E. Sanford Company 1049 South Hill Street Los Angeles 15, Calif.	D. E. Sanford Company 12th and Howard Streets San Francisco 3, Calif.	R. T. Carson 600 Merchandise Mart Kansas City 8, Mo.
	D. E. Sanford Company Merchandise Mart, 1931 Second Avenue Seattle 1, Wash.	Lee Kennedy 3500 Ridgewood Road, N.W. Atlanta, Ga.	

(ucago)

Blue Ridge dinnerware advertisement, *China, Glass and Decorative Accessories Magazine,* June 1951.

AMERICAN-MADE SEMI-PORCELA IN
Popular Tableware
COMMANDS ATTENTION AND WINS SALES

Hand Painted Under Glaze!

12 Styles Semi-Porcelain 9 In. Salad Bowls

- 12 colorful, American-made semi-porcelain bowls . . . each one with a different design.
- Eye-appealing flower and fruit patterns . . . hand painted under protective, beautifying glaze.
- In a popular size . . . 9 inches overall diameter.
- Unaffected priorities . . . plenty of merchandise for you to sell.
- Used every day . . . in demand the year around.
- Merchandise that presents real value to your customers . . . and offers big profit opportunities for you!

When you order these salad bowls by the dozen here's the extraordinary value you get: 12 hand painted bowls, each with a different flower or fruit pattern . . . the RIGHT assortment to make your selling job easier than ever before. Each bowl in the group is designed to please ALL customers. Multiply that satisfaction by 12 and the answer is a world of greater customer acceptance. Sell these salad bowls with a minimum of effort . . . and buy with confidence backed by Butlers guarantee of best possible quality at the price.
55R-422—3 doz in carton. 48 lbs..................Doz 2.20

$2.20 DOZ

Extra Fancy 9 Inch Salad Bowls . . . 6 Under-Glaze Hand Painted Patterns

Elaborately hand painted American-made semi-porcelain bowls in 6 equally assorted floral and fruit patterns that are sure to win their way into your customers' kitchens. Attractively shaped, measure 9 in. in diameter.
55R-423—3 doz in carton. 48 lbs............

The hand painting is artistically applied under glaze . . . won't wear off. The patterns are pleasing, colorful and decorative . . . just to look at them explains their sales attraction. Make this assortment YOUR best seller!
.........................Doz 2.50

$2.50 Doz

Extra Fancy 10 Inch Bowls . . . 3 Hand Painted Patterns

Elaborately decorated American-made semi-porcelain salad bowls, large in size and appealing in design. 3 hand painted patterns, assorted 2 floral and 1 fruit. The painted decoration is applied under protective, beautifying glaze to give this tableware lasting attractiveness.
55R-424—1 doz in carton, 19 lbs............Doz 3.60

$3.60 Doz

8½ Inch Deep Shaped Salad Bowls

Here's an attractive bowl made of domestic semi-porcelain with colorful green maroon design stamped in center and assorted green and pink tinted borders. Measures 8½ in. in diameter, has deep shape.
55R-431—3 doz in pkg, 40 lbs...**Doz 1.65**

9½ Inch Bowls with Floral Centers

Unusually colorful bowl with blue stamped floral center pattern and lustrous background in assorted shades of brown and green. Wide bowl, 9½ in. in diameter, made of American semi-porcelain.
55R-406—2 doz in pkg, 35 lbs...**Doz 2.00**

Colorfully Designed 9½ Inch Bowls

Lovely floral pattern stamped in center, attractive border. Assorted colors of rose border with green center, yellow with blue and green with rose center. Made of American semi-porcelain, 9½ in. in diam.
55R-433—2 doz in ctn, 35 lbs....**Doz 2.10**

9 Inch Bowls with Appealing Floral Pattern

American-made semi-porcelain, stamped floral center design, embossed and sprayed border. Color combinations as follows: Blue border with green center, pink with pink, yellow with blue center, equally asstd. to ctn.
55R-411—2 doz in ctn, 35 lbs.....**Doz 2.10**

Tableware shown in Butler Bros. catalog in 1952.

BLUE RIDGE
D I N N E R W A R E

No. 4261 Skyline

Charm for the

Children too!

Blue Ridge parades perky Mr. Duck and his family, all dressed up in their Sunday best, across this enticing Child's Set. The pleasant personality of these playmates makes every meal an exciting event.

Hand Painted, like all Blue Ridge Ware, the Underglaze decoration remains fresh and bright through years of service.

So nice to take home and a gift of good taste, for any member of the tricycle crowd.

*S*outhern *P*otteries, *I*nc.
Erwin, Tennessee
Representatives

Cox & Company
208 Fifth Ave.
New York 10, N. Y.

Lee Kennedy
3500 Ridgewood Road, N.W.
Atlanta, Ga.

Earl W. Newton & Associates
1563 Merchandise Mart
Chicago 54, Ill.

United Potteries Co.
Renkert Bldg.
Canton 2, Ohio

United China & Glass Co.
400-420 Canal Street
New Orleans 6, La.

United China & Glass Co.
10th Floor, Second Unit
Santa Fe Bldg.
Dallas, Texas

R. T. Carson
600 Merchandise Mart
Kansas City 8, Mo.

D. E. Sanford Co.
12th & Howard Streets
San Francisco 3, Calif.

D. E. Sanford Co.
1049 South Hill St.
Los Angeles 15, Calif.

D. E. Sanford Co.
Merchandise Mart
1931 Second Ave.
Seattle 1, Wash.

61

Advertisement for Blue Ridge dinnerware for children, No. 4261 Skyline.

Blue Ridge Skyline appeared in *House Beautiful* in 1951. Patterns shown are "Plantation Ivy" (above) and "Bittersweet" (below).

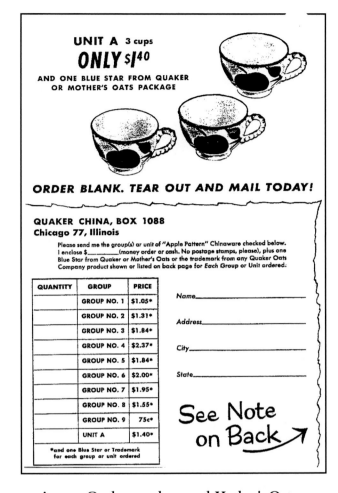

Pamphlet for "Apple" pattern chinaware offered as a premium on Quaker products and Mother's Oats.

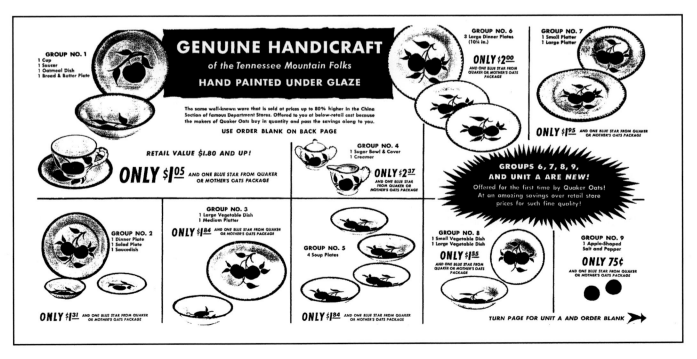

This Blue Ridge pattern was used in this Carnation Milk advertisement which appeared in *Good Housekeeping,* February 1947.

Color advertisement for Blue Ridge featuring color on color designs. Patterns shown are #4333 "Night Flower" and #4332 "Golden Sands" on Skyline.

Pictured with this article from *The American Home* is Southern Potteries' "Colonial" china on a picnic table. Magazine is dated September 1942.

SETS YOU CAN COLLECT

We get lots of letters from collectors asking us "what pieces were made in my pattern?" Usually, the answer is "everything!" Following are a few photos showing what you may find when you hunt.

The "Valley Violet" Breakfast Set in its entirety.

More pieces of "Bluebell Bouquet." Remember that some pieces have two or more upright green leaves and some have upright yellow leaves.

A selection of pieces in "Bluebell Bouquet" pattern.

"Crab Apple" will be found on a myriad of pieces. Southern Potteries' employees have told us that "Crab Apple" was the most popular pattern they had.

More and more pieces are turning up in "Red Barn" pattern.

Lucky is the collector who amasses this selection of "Swiss Dancers" pattern.

Here are a couple of views from the Annual Blue Ridge Show and Sale held each year in Erwin, Tennessee, home of Southern Potteries. Collectors visiting it for the first time are overwhelmed! In 1996, the show moved to a larger and prettier location, so things can only get better!

Here we are at the show — Bill and I — having a grand time as usual.

The Unicoi Heritage Museum (left). The old dining room of the house is used as a showcase for Blue Ridge dinnerware, sponsored by the Blue Ridge Pottery Club in Erwin (below).

FAKES & REPRODUCTIONS

One can always tell when a collectible has "made it" into the higher brackets — folks start making reproductions of it. Blue Ridge has not escaped this phenomenon. Back in 1985, the first reproduction Character Jugs came on the market. They bore the Blue Ridge logo on the base, but were in earthenware rather than porcelain. A number of vases, pitchers, and teapots followed, mainly in shapes never made by Southern Potteries except for the Rebecca and Milady shapes. The painting on these pieces was inferior to the art of Southern Potteries and in size they were somewhat larger.

Since the 1980s and currently in production are a great many Blue Ridge look-alikes made by the Erwin Pottery in Erwin, Tennessee. Since the reproductions were exposed, we have been finding the word "Repro" added to the Blue Ridge backstamp, or the words "Original Blue Ridge Pattern, SPI, Erwin Pottery." Sometimes the pieces have only the initials N.P. on them which stands for Negatha Peterson, owner of Erwin Pottery. Be sure to check your marks and the shape of the pieces very carefully. Know your Blue Ridge shapes!

The easiest way to determine a Character Jugs reproduction is to examine the inside of the jug where the handle attaches to the main body. If there is a hole, top and/or bottom indicating that the handle is molded in one piece with the body, you have a reproduction. The original porcelain jug handles were attached or applied, which keeps the inside of the jug smooth.

Keep in mind also that Southern Potteries was primarily a dinnerware maker so items like wall pockets, planters, spoon rests, etc. will not be Southern Potteries products.

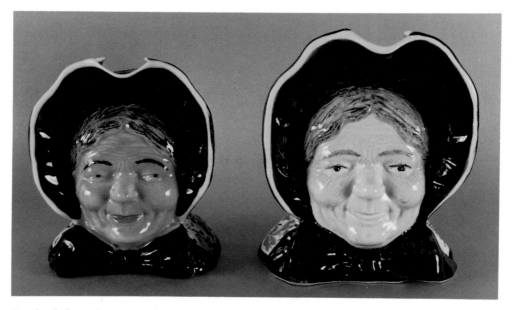

On the left is the original Southern Potteries Pioneer Woman Character Jug. She is done in porcelain. On the right is a Pioneer Woman done by the Cash Family's Clinchfield Artware Pottery. Notice the difference in size; this is because the porcelain base material shrinks more in the making than the earthenware.

On the left is Paul Revere by the Cash Family. On the right is Daniel Boone by Southern Potteries. Notice the hole in the top handle of Paul Revere. This is a fast way to decide if the piece is really Southern or not. The porcelain Character Jugs made by Southern Potteries have applied handles, thus there is no hole which is made by shrinkage of the molded-in-one handle.

One of the "Blue Ridge look-alikes" made by Erwin Pottery's Negatha Peterson. Notice the original Blue Ridge stamp that she used in the beginning. This is not a Blue Ridge shape, either.

Another vase made by Erwin Pottery to look like Blue Ridge (left); this shape was never made by Southern. It is 4½" tall. Notice the mark on the bottom of this vase (right); after many collector complaints, Mrs. Peterson began adding the word "Repro" to her stamp. Since then, she has added several more different logos.

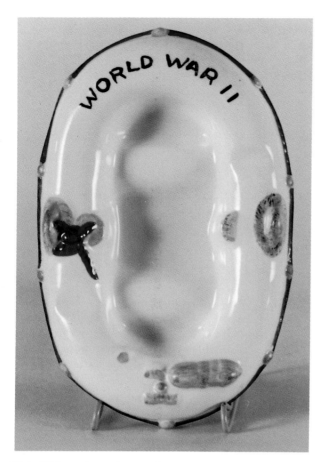

This 7" long boat is another Southern Potteries fake. I hate the word "fake," but that is all I can call it. Although Southern Potteries' mark is used, this is not one of their pieces. Who the culprit is, we don't know.

SOUTHERN? STETSON? SOMEBODY?

How many times have you picked up a piece of lovely, hand-painted dinnerware just certain it must be Blue Ridge and found the name "Stetson" on the back? Or perhaps you have run across the seemingly common greenish Dogwood pattern, with little red/brown dots on the edge of each petal, shaped like Blue Ridge, painted liked Blue Ridge, but what does one find on the back? "Joni," that's what! We have found this to be a mark used by Stetson for a special customer of theirs. We tried for years to track down the maker of this china, but found only plates, which were on a blank just like Southern's Skyline.

Finally we found a set with cups and there was the distinctive Stetson handle. Watch for these "different" handles on hollow ware items if you are uncertain as to manufacturer. Again, know your Southern Potteries shapes. Stetson finials are also distinctive, one being a rather modernistic spiral shape. Some line or shape names occasionally found on Stetson ware are Rio, Heritage, and American Heritage.

Stetson also had glassware painted to match some of its patterns, especially "Dogwood." One box of tumblers we found was marked "Mar-Crest Manufacturing Co., Chicago, Illinois," which we believe was a special logo used for items produced for and sold by Marshall Field and Co. in Chicago.

Stetson was located in Lincoln, Illinois, from 1946 to 1966. Louis Stetson was a Polish immigrant working in Chicago. He heard a good business opportunity was buying whiteware, decorating, and re-selling it. He bought his first whiteware from Mt. Clemens Pottery with Mt. Clemens financing the venture. His business prospered and he brought his nephew, Joe, from Poland to help. Louis died after a few years and Joe took over the business, Mt. Clemens could not supply enough ware and Joe began buying from the Illinois China Company in Lincoln. By 1946, business had grown to such an extent he purchased the Illinois China plant. Buying odd lots of decals and otherwise cutting corners, he was able to give a good price to his customers and the business prospered.

In the mid 1950s, he discontinued decal decorating in favor of hand painting. He brought decorators in from the faltering Southern Potteries and Redwing Pottery. Lena Watts, who was head decorator-designer at Southern for many years, moved to Stetson also, which accounts for the many look-alike patterns produced by Stetson during that time.

In 1955, they advertised themselves as the "largest manufacturer of hand-painted dinnerware in the U.S." By that time, with Southern on its last legs, it was probably true. However, hand painting only lasted two or three years at Stetson, and they returned to the use of decals. Almost all the later production was sold to brokerage firms who bought items to sell to furniture and grocery stores for premiums. As with Blue Ridge, much of Stetson's product was not marked.

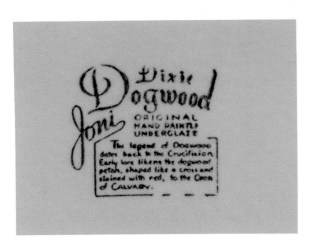

This is the mark found on the Stetson "Dixie Dogwood" pattern. Note the red dots on the ends of the petals (right).

Another Stetson mark, used on a stylized rooster pattern.

OTHER TENNESSEE POTTERIES

Eastern Tennessee, where Blue Ridge originated, has a long history of pottery making beginning with the family potteries of the nineteenth century who manufactured the utilitarian redware pieces necessary to every family of the time. There were jugs for whiskey and molasses syrup, churns, bowls of all sizes, milk pans, crocks, pitchers, all types of preserving jars, and crocks for sauerkraut and other food-stuffs.

Most of the old potters used an above ground, circular updraft kiln, which resembled an Eskimo igloo with one door and a small hole in the top. A few square or rectangular kilns were also used, along with an occasional "bee-hive" kiln. This redware was produced at some sites late into the nineteenth century.

The availability of local clays was one of the reasons for the many "jug potteries" in middle and eastern Tennessee. Being a potter in those early days was a lot of hard work! First, they had to find a deposit of the right kind of clay. Then it was dug by hand with picks and shovels, loaded onto a horse-drawn wagon and taken to drying sheds built near the kiln. Once dried, it was ground and mixed in a clay mill. The pottery pieces were thrown on a homemade kick wheel or treadle wheel. Sometimes a potter hired a "turner" or skilled potter to make the ware. A kiln load took him 14 to 17 days to throw. The turner also stacked the vessels in the kiln, as proper stacking was very important to the finished product. For his labors, he generally received one-quarter to one-third of the profits from a kiln load.

Just firing the kiln was laborious. The family chopped wood all year — mainly oak and hickory. There were two steps to firing a kiln. First, a small fire was built in the lower chamber of the fire box which allowed the temperature to rise at an even rate. The proper temperature was reached usually in three full days and required four to five cords of wood. Small test pieces of clay were put into the loaded kiln and used to determine whether the stoneware was sufficiently fired. After this, 300 to 500 very dry hardwood rails or poles, four to six-inches thick and eight feet long, were placed in the upper chamber of the kiln fire box, which had been sealed with bricks during the first firing. Handfuls of salt were then thrown through the lower and middle holes in the kiln, using 60 to 80 pounds of salt for each firing. At this extreme heat, the salt would vaporize instantly, leaving a clear glaze on the vessels. After approximately three more days and nights of cooling, the loading door was finally opened and the ware removed. About ten percent breakage was considered normal.

Local folks came to the kiln to buy their pieces, but most of the ware was sold by one or two men traveling in a horse or mule drawn wagon for up to 10 days at a time. Even then, payment was not always money, but often groceries, meat, eggs, etc.

It was from this tradition of pottery making that the modern-day potteries evolved — big potteries like Southern Potteries in Erwin, Tennessee; smaller potteries like Cash Family Clinchfield Artware, Cherokee Pottery, and Clouse Pottery.

CHEROKEE POTTERY

In the early 1940s, G.F. Brandt moved from Erwin, Tennessee, where he was associated with the Southern Potteries, to Jonesboro to establish the Cherokee China Company. I understand the building was constructed by Dan and Ray Cash, of the Cash Family Potteries. With the help of Brandt's two sons, Fritz and Frederich, the Cherokee Pottery operations continued for 10 to 12 years. Evidently at some point, they moved to Rogersville, Tennessee, as some of their marks indicate.

The firm produced a molded, underglaze, hand-painted whiteware. They made dishes, flower vases, pitchers, and miniature knick-knacks, all hand decorated. Marks shown are stamped in black ink.

CHEROKEE POTTERY
ROGERSVILLE, TENN.
HAND PAINTED
("Hand painted" is in smaller letters.)

A label in metallic red with silver, showing an Indian has also been found. This label is marked:

Cherokee
Jonesboro, Tenn.

Pitchers: 4½" "Pointed-Leaf Ivy" (left); 3¼" "Pointed-Leaf Ivy" (center), 3" "Pansy" (right).

4⅝" unmarked pitcher but carries the Cherokee label.

7" earthenware pitcher, marked.

4¾" souvenir pitcher, marked "Shenandoah Valley, Va." (left); 5" souvenir pitcher, marked "Montreat, NC" (right).

8½" tall fan vase.

5½" tall teapot, has same red flower on other side, plus two small blue flowers.

6" Pitcher-vase, porcelain, marked (left); cornucopia vase, 6¾" tall, 6" wide at base (right).

7½" Betsy-type jug, marked "hand painted."

Red and silver label showing Indian figure and the words "Cherokee Jonesboro, Tenn."

BUFFALO POTTERY

Buffalo Pottery was started by Walter and Pauline Mountford at their home in Erwin, Tennessee, about 1967. Pauline was a decorator at Southern Potteries, and we're told she was "the fastest painter they had." Walter modeled the buffalo used at the Buffalo Golf Course near Erwin. The pottery operated for only about 2½ years.

Buffalo Pottery mark.

Log-shaped butterdish.

CLOUSE (UNAKA) POTTERY

Information provided by Eleanor Clouse Fondren.

Date Clouse was a jiggerman at Southern Potteries and his wife, Bonnie, was a hand-painter. During World War II, Date left Southern for a stint in the Navy. Upon his return, around 1946, they started their own pottery about a mile and a half out of Erwin. They called this business Unaka Pottery.

Clouse's produced a cream colored, translucent porcelain ware using slip Date mixed himself out of mostly locally mined material. Bonnie's sister, Lena Watts, did the designing, and she and Bonnie together took care of the hand painting. You will remember that Lena Watts was also Southern Potteries' head decorator until she moved to Stetson Pottery in Illinois.

Unaka Pottery produced a large variety of items, such as souvenir pieces, vases, powder boxes, baby booties, baby mugs, tiny shoes, western boots, large pitchers, etc. In some pieces the finished porcelain was so thin, one would almost see through it when held to the light.

Date and Bonnie loved the pottery, even with all its hard work, and they were in business for about 10 years. The same conditions that forced Southern Potteries to close also affected Unaka Pottery. After the war, the market was flooded with goods from Japan and other countries and the American potteries could no longer make a profit.

Many Clouse pieces are marked, but some are not; since they are so similar to Cherokee Pottery items, it is difficult to tell which is which. Marks used are as follows, stamped in black ink.

**CLOUSE
HAND PAINTED
CHINA**

**CLOUSE
HAND PAINTED**

*Clouse
Hand Painted
Artware*

Bonnie and Date Clouse in front of their Unaka pottery building.

4¼" square pitcher with "Pansies," marked "Hand Painted, Gatlinburg, Tenn."

2½" tall ruffle-top pot with "Violas" (left); 4¼" square pitcher with "Pointed-Leaf Ivy" (right).

Several 2" tall mini pitchers. Left to right: "Pine Cone," "Pansy" marked "Natural Chimneys, Va.", "Pointed Leaf Ivy" marked "Fountain of Youth, St. Augustine, Fla.," and "Bleeding Heart" pattern.

4⅛" "Pink Dogwood" pitcher (left); 3½" jug marked "The Big Apple, Hotel Crisfield" (right).

2¾" diameter pin box.

7" flared top vase (left); 4½" pitcher (right).

5¼" cache pot vase (left); 2½" small ruffled pot (right).

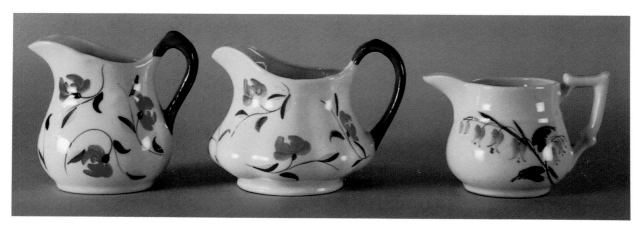

4" pitcher (left) and 3¾" pitcher (center) are marked "Hand Painted, Fontana Dam, N.C." 3⅛" pitcher (right) is marked "Hand Painted, Souvenir of Shenandoah Valley."

Left: Cup and saucer, demi size. Cup 2¼" tall, saucer 4½" diameter. Marked "Hand Painted, Fontana Dam, N.C." Right: 3⅛" pitcher, marked "Hand Painted, Souvenir of Shenandoah Valley."

2⅜" diameter pin box, marked "Hand Painted, Underglaze."

Pitchers marked "Natural Bridge, Va." 3¾" tall "Pointed-Leaf Ivy" (left); 3¾" "Pansy" (right).

Two 4⅛" pitchers: "Pansy" (left); "Pointed-Leaf Ivy" (right).

3¼" tall "Pine Tree" pitcher (left), 2⅞" pin box (center), 3¼" "Dogwood" pitcher (right).

Individual size creamer and sugar in "Pansy."

Assortment of Clouse pieces including a small pin tray marked "Nancy Johnson, 1954–55." Notice also the tiny shoe on the left.

Pair of baby booties marked "Texie."

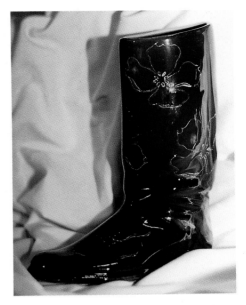

Cobalt blue tall boot. I understand Mr. Clouse mixed this color himself. Notice the dogwood flowers incised into the paint. This is a one-of-a-kind article.

Two strawberry pitchers marked "Shenandoah, Va." plus a teeny pitcher with one little rosebud in the foreground.

THE UNDECIDEDS

Unless the piece is clearly marked, we have found that distinguishing Cherokee china from Clouse (Unaka) china is very difficult. With about 50 pieces, marked and unmarked, in front of us, we were determined to find a common denominator. First, we checked patterns; the distinctive spade-leafed vines, the red-flowered pieces with brown edges and handles, and the pansies. No luck there, as we found all these decorations on both marked Clouse and on marked Cherokee. Shape — that should tell. The fancy handles on several pieces; the pointy spout, the body shapes; still no luck. Identical shapes were discovered in both. One authority states that Clouse's production was porcelain whereas Cherokee produced earthenware. After checking all 50 pieces, we discovered that it was true that the main body of the Clouse pieces was porcelain, but some of the Cherokee items were also!

Surely, we thought, there would be some distinguishing feature about the marks themselves. One pottery probably marked in block letters, one in script. We found a variety of type styles used interchangeably by both. The same thing held true with colors used in decorating. Both potteries seem to have used the same color spectrum.

Finally, we came to the conclusion that unless pieces are marked as to pottery of origin, there is no easy or sure way to tell them apart. We just have to collect both and love them equally for what they are; beautiful, high-quality, well-made ware that will delight any pottery lover. If any readers find a foolproof method to tell them apart, we would love to hear about it. The following photos illustrate the "Undecided Origin" pieces — either Clouse or Cherokee, but which is which remains a mystery.

7⅜" tall handled vase.

Two earthenware unmarked pitchers.

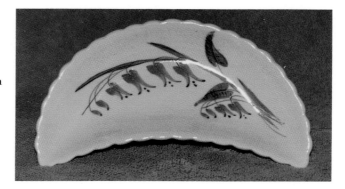

Scalloped edge bone dish with "Bleeding Heart."

Left to right: 3¼" shaker, 3" covered sugar, 3¾" creamer, matching 3¼" shaker. Colors resemble Cherokee more than Clouse.

Earthenware pitcher, unknown shape.

5" pitcher marked "Lake Junaluska, N.C." (left); 4¼" square pitcher marked "Hand Painted Watts Bar Village" (right).

3¾" "Pansy" pitcher marked "Hand Painted, Gatlinburg, Tenn." (left); 4" "White Dogwood" porcelain pitcher, no mark (right).

6⅜" bone dish, marked on front "Chimney Rock, N.C."; on bottom, "Hand Painted Chimney Rock, N.C." (left). Pin box, earthenware rather than porcelain, marked "Souvenir Silver Springs, Fla." (right).

2⅝" pitcher (left); 3⅜" jug marked "Hand Painted, Gatlinburg, Tenn." (center); 1⅞" creamer also marked "Hand Painted, Gatlinburg, Tenn." (right).

Two mini pitchers, 2⅜" tall: porcelain (left); earthenware (right).

THE CASH FAMILY
CLINCHFIELD ARTWARE POTTERY

Ray and Pauline Cash began Clinchfield Artware in 1945 in a small building behind their home in Erwin, Tennessee. They began making three pieces of pottery. These were the rolling pin planter, the small elephant pitcher, and the buttermilk jug. The clay was mixed in their old-fashioned washing machine, a small kiln fired the pieces, the oven of their kitchen stove dried the molds, and Pauline went on the road selling these first three pieces. From this beginning, Clinchfield Artware had grown in 1979 to 21 employees, including Ray and Pauline's son and daughter-in-law. Two electric kilns were in operation and were fired four times a day during busy seasons. Two smaller electric and one large oil-fired kiln were used now and then.

After the first, or bisque firing which is 2,395° and takes about four hours, the pieces are removed from the kiln and stamped with the Clinchfield Artware trademark. Several different marks were used interchangeably depending on the customer's preference or "how we happened to feel that day," Mrs. Cash told us. One mark bears the 1945 beginning date. After stamping, the foot of the piece is waxed to prevent sticking during final firing.

Next, it's to the decorating shop where a number of artists, including several who worked at one time or another for Southern Potteries, do their magic with fruits, flowers, and birds. After decorating, the pieces are hand-dipped in the glaze tub and fired again in the glaze kiln at 1600° for about five hours. During firing, the opaque glaze becomes transparent — actually turns to glass — and all "runs" and "sags" disappear.

Many of the molds used were Cash Family designs. Quite a few molds were purchased from Southern Potteries when they liquidated. Others are reproductions of antique pieces, such as the popular buttermilk pitcher, and still more were purchased from other now-defunct potteries. At their peak, Clinchfield Artware claimed an inventory of 5,000 pieces. They did not make dinnerware; their production was specialty and souvenir pieces.

Ray and Pauline Cash in front of the pottery building.

Decorators at work at Clinchfield Artware Pottery.

Loading the kiln at Clinchfield Artware Pottery.

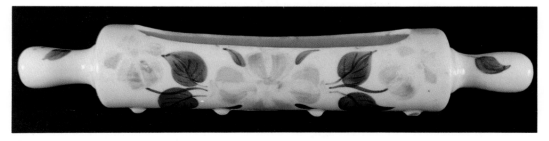

This is the rolling pin planter that was one of the first items made by the Cashes.

Duck or mallard pitcher, 9" tall.

5½" tall Toby Jug.

Cash Family version of the Betsy Jug.

Counter sign for Clinchfield Artware made just like the counter sign that Southern Potteries used for Blue Ridge.

Another of the Cashes' first items was this elephant pitcher which Shawnee collectors will recognize as a replica of theirs (left). Hand bud vase — an early piece also (right).

Two color variations of the 11¼" tall "Oak Leaf & Acorn" vase.

The popular 13½" long Piggy Bank. Cash would paint these for customers using their choice of decoration plus the name and date for the "Birthday Person."

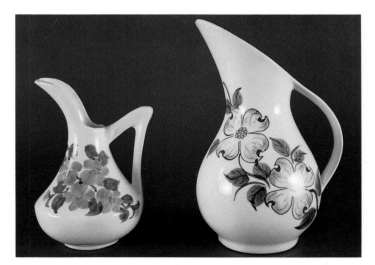

5½" blue-flowered pitcher (left), 8¼" "Dogwood" pitcher (right).

Cash version of the Chick Pitcher first made by Southern Potteries.

Small 3" tall, 3-spouted pitcher (left); 7½" Buttermilk Pitcher (right). This was a big seller for Cash and will be found with many different decorations.

4" "Violet" decorated pitcher with "Townsend, Tenn." on back (left); 3⅛" squatty jug (center); 5" stylized "Dogwood" pitcher (right).

CLINCHFIELD ARTWARE POTTERY MARKS

Late Cash mark

PRICING FOR THE SMALL POTTERIES

Since the smaller East Tennessee potteries are just now beginning to attract collectors, we can only give a preliminary pricing idea.

Small pieces: 1" to 2½" high $5.00–10.00
Medium pieces: 3" to 4" high $10.00–15.00
Large pieces: 4" to 8" high $15.00–20.00
Fancy pieces: *(cornucopias, fan vases, etc.)* $30.00–45.00

Since the collecting of the Cash Family Clinchfield Artware is really in its infancy, and since these pieces are mainly not as old as Cherokee or Clouse, a price range has not been established.

DID YOU KNOW...?

That demi or after dinner size sugars and creamers seem to be more difficult to find than demi pots, cups, and saucers? And that china demi sets are the most elusive of all?

That the "Dogtooth Violet" handled vase has been found in plain orange lustre, believed to be made earlier in Clinchfield ware?

That the white gift boxes used for china sugar and creamer sets and china chocolate pots were especially made for Southern Potteries in Bristol, Tennessee?

That china shakers are sometimes marked "Blue Ridge China" and sometimes not marked at all?

That the "Rock Rose" pattern comes with either pink or yellow roses?

That silicosis, sometimes called "Black Lung" and usually considered a miner's disease, also affected pottery workers? It is caused by rock dust, I'm told, and some died from it.

That Southern Potteries made only one boot vase, the 8" size? Smaller and larger boots are products of Spaulding China.

That one Southern Potteries jiggerman (the man who shapes flatware on a potter's wheel) claimed his output was 240 dozen pieces a day?

That the Palace Theater mentioned on the "Your Gift From The Palace, Pixie" tray was located in Erwin, Tennessee?

That squatty sherbets and double egg cups have been found matching several patterns?

That the larger end of the double egg cup was introduced for folks who did not like to eat their egg straight from the shell? They could now scoop the egg out of the shell and sometimes combine it with bits of toast, this all being mixed together in the larger end of the cup.

That lamps and wall sconces have been found made from teapots, coffee pots, and in the case of the sconces, a plate and cup? Keep in mind that while Southern Potteries made all the pottery pieces for these items, they were sold to other manufacturers who fitted them with the metal parts.

That Southern Potteries was mainly a dinnerware producer with a few very decorative items made in fine china? They did not make novelty items, such as wall pockets, planters, pie birds, sprinkler bottles, etc.

That one style of the Blue Ridge salad fork was made from the same mold as the matching salad spoon, with the fork tines being cut out of the end of the spoon?

That if the decorative item you find is painted over the glaze (feel with your fingernail), then it is not Blue Ridge?

That an 11½" "Lyonnaise" plate has been found on a Candlewick blank?

That decorated-to-match glassware of the same shape as that decorated for Blue Ridge was also made for the E. M. Knowles China Company and for Metlox China to name just a few?

That there is a gray "Spiderweb" pattern as well as pink, aqua, and maybe others?

That mixing bowl sets come in 5¾", 6¾", 7½", and 9" sizes?

That a "coupe" soup bowl is the shape name that a number of potteries gave to deep but smaller around soup/cereal bowls that have a handle or a vestige of a handle on both sides of the bowl, as opposed to a "flat soup" which is shallower and larger in diameter?

That the Erwin Pottery in Erwin, Tennessee, is making loads of Blue Ridge "look-alikes," sometimes marked with Blue Ridge marks and sometimes with their own mark and sometimes even with just the owner's initials, N.P.?

That pictures featuring Blue Ridge will often be found in old cookbooks and illustrating the food articles in old magazines? The furniture sections of old Sears and Ward catalogs often have Blue Ridge on the shelves or tables shown for sale.

That the Chick Pitcher has also been found with a souvenir motto and made by Clouse Pottery?

That after extensive tests, Blue Ridge dinnerware has been shown not to leach lead?

That the Deviled Egg Dish made by Southern Potteries is quite rounded on the bottom side and has no foot ring and only a very small flat area in the center, while imported egg dishes are very flat on the bottom with the foot ring coming within 1½–2" from the outer edge?

That the S. P. Co. mark was used by Superior Porcelain Company of Parkersburg, West Virginia? Southern Potteries' products always say S.P. Inc., or SPI or SPI Inc. written out in script.

That the curved pieces of the Southern Potteries Lazy Susan do not have lids — only the center bowl is covered?

That flexible aquarium tubing cut into correct lengths will pad your metal plate hangers and reduce the danger of damaging the plate?

That the Dorothy Bon-bon, Rebecca, Jane, Alice, Sally, etc., pitchers, Martha relishes and such are not artist names — they are shape names?

That there are two rim patterns on French Peasant pieces; one has the leaf garland with red flowers and blue berries. The other has the leaf garland alternating blue and orange flowers with no berries?

That Cake Plates are fairly flat, generally squared in shape and have handles molded from the body?

That Chop Plates, Serving Plates or Underplates measure 12½" to 14" in diameter and have no handles?

That a tray is identified as a piece made to have other pieces sitting on it such as the chocolate set, waffle set or demi sets?

That Betsy Jugs will be found in both china and earthenware?

That the Martha Jug has been identified as the paneled shape quite like the china Grace Jug, except in plain colors and with highly raised and sculpted scrollwork?

That a Nude Dancers shape box has been found done in all-over light green and marked "Germany?"

VOICES FROM THE PAST

Excerpt from "A Century of American Dinnerware" by Floyd McKee, 1963:

Southern Potteries at Erwin, Tennessee, established in 1918, was born because of the idea that the Carolina, Clinchfield & Ohio Railroad should get some industries going that would help bring some traffic into the Johnson City area. Ted Owens, late of Minerva, Ohio, went down there to build it in the early 1910s. The task of keeping old potters down there and training the boys from the hills was too much for him and it had to be reorganized a couple of times. Charles Foreman from Minerva happened along and took a try at it. Not too much progress was made in attaining a quality piece of ware, but by introducing hand-painting on the bisque by the crew method, much as hand filled prints had been colored, and coupling this with the low wages accepted by the girls from back in the mountains, it made the grade. It sold simple patterns at as little as $5.50 per "L" to such promoters of theater premiums as Jake Price. World War II came along and the patterns were improved as well as the workmanship and they were "off to the races." Foreman and Foster Hankins of Lexington, North Dakota, who for years had jobbed ware under the name of Foster Pottery Co., were principal stockholders. Foster had a 25 per cent interest and got a fancy figure from his partners. This stopped him from annoying the others by continually urging them to sell out to various people who needed the output of a pottery in their business. I believe five million was offered for it at one time. The mode of operation permitted the withdrawal of one pattern and the issuance of a new one with a minimum of expense and trouble. The OPA was never very good about following the complications of the pottery business and the plant proved quite a gold mine. Charles Foreman continued to maintain a sales agency in Canton, Ohio, that he had when he took over Southern, controlling the distribution of a good part of the output. His health was very poor for years and winters were spent at Ft. Lauderdale, Florida. His death occurred in 1953. A decision was made to liquidate the operation in January, 1957. Hugh Kibler took over the management on Foreman's death and did a good job of liquidation, finally selling the plant to the National Casket Co. of Boston, who are using the plant for the production of metallic caskets.

On January 31, 1957, the *ERWIN RECORD* put out an extra edition. The headlines were "Southern Potteries Stockholders Vote to Close Plant." A sub-heading informed folks that "Directors Will Meet Feb. 7 To Arrange Sale of All Assets. Say Potteries' Customers Will be Given Chance to Stock Up On Patterns."

"Stockholders of Southern Potteries, Inc., voted Tuesday afternoon to liquidate the firm." The brief announcement concerning the stockholders action was released to this newspaper Wednesday afternoon by H. W. Kibler, president and general manager, and Roland Sevier.

The stockholder's decision called for Southern Potteries to liquidate as quickly and as economically as possible. A committee will be appointed next week to carry out the liquidation, Mr. Sevier said.

Southern Potteries, Inc., is Erwin's biggest industry and is reported to have the largest payroll here. Head of the local potters union has been notified of the action.

As to how the closing out of Southern Potteries business in Erwin will be carried out will not be learned until after the board of directors meets February 7. Offers are expected from outside sources and they may prove a boon to the county. Next week's meeting is important, as all concerned seem to agree.

Southern Potteries still has a backlog of orders from various firms. It was reported by several stockholders that various large mail order houses and trading stamp premium firms will be given the opportunity to stock up on patterns currently being offered. Several mail order firms have Southern Potteries dinnerware listed in new catalogs and they may wish to lay in a supply.

It is hoped by some observers that the disposition can be made of the property to some large industry which might possibly employ a larger labor force.

Unicoi County's Industrial Committee immediately got in contact with G. A. Bentley, the county's industrial commissioner who is in Cleveland, to inform him of the local development.

From a local newspaper column dated 1946:

Thousands on top of thousands of dishes are made in Erwin, Tennessee each day — all of them hand painted by 500 girls of the area at the foot of the Great Smokies.

Half of Southern Potteries Incorporated 1,000 employees are girls who paint (or decorate) the dishes on a production line basis. No special training is required before starting to fill in minor details on the ware. As they gain experience, they are moved up to painting the more intricate parts of flowers and other figures in the designs.

But despite the size of the factory — it's the largest of its kind in the country — and despite the production line basis of the decorators' work, the job apparently doesn't get monotonous, for patterns and jobs are changed frequently. Starting to work in the morning a girl may paint the stem of a flower; late in the day, she will paint the leaf on another kind of flower and still later fill in the petals on still another design.

Practically all the patterns the company uses were originated at the plant, the chief designer being a native of Erwin with more than 1,000 models to her credit.

The pottery has 3,800 different patterns which can be reproduced without too much trouble, but now has in production only some 400.

Organized in 1918, Southern Potteries at first made only general pottery ware. Eight years ago, however, the plant started all-out production of hand-painted dinnerware, china specialties, and utility items. since then it has grown from a 175-employee concern and has made its "Blue Ridge" trademark known throughout the world. The South's only manufacturer of its kind, it now turns out over 324,000 single pieces of ware each week — and that's a lot of plates.

Surprisingly enough the raw materials do not come from the area, but most of the clay is shipped from various sections of Georgia, North Carolina and Tennessee and is mixed at the plant.

Technically speaking, the products are known as "underglaze, hand-painted semi-porcelain dinnerware" and "underglaze, hand-painted china specialties and utility items." This means that the design is painted on the plate before it is given its slick finish, or glaze, so that no matter how often the dish is washed or how hot the foods placed on it, the color can not come off.

The mixed clay is shaped by plaster of paris molds, large hand stamps and on wheels. For 48 hours it is baked at 2,100 degrees F. in a bisque kiln. Then it goes to the decorating rooms, and after decoration gets an application of glaze compound and another baking.

Though the kilns are in continuous operation, most of the workers, members of the National Brotherhood of Operative Potters (A.F.L.) are on the job a straight 40 hours a week. The plant is unionized but not a closed shop.

Postwar plans of the company are not complete, but include expansion and the addition of a new tunnel kiln to the four now in operation.

From the Clinchfield Goodwill Edition newspaper in 1940:

POTTERY EXAMPLE OF CLINCHFIELD ROUTE INFLUENCE IN BRINGING NEW INDUSTRIES

The influence of the Clinchfield Route in bringing other industrial plants to Erwin can be felt strongly through the location of Southern Potteries here in 1917, eight years after the railroad set up its shops and yard.

Erwin, with its surrounding natural resources, was a logical location point for such an industry, of course, but without the facilities of a railroad, the pottery might as well have picked a spot in the middle of a desert.

Twenty-three years after starting operation in Erwin, Southern Potteries is keeping step with industrial paces by gradually enlarging in order to fill inrushing orders.

Work will soon start on a giant, new circular tunnel kiln, one which will step up output of the plant 40 percent. It will be the third such kiln constructed in five years, replacing old slower and non-mechanized kilns. Approximately $30,000 will be expended.

A spokesman of the pottery made the announcement of the addition recently but was unable to determine the number of new employees that would be needed after its completion.

Southern Potteries employ 340 and has an annual payroll of approximately $450,000 or from $35,000 to $40,000 each month. The plant works seven days a week and 24 hours a day. In the neighborhood of 3,000 dozen pieces of dinnerware and other products are turned out daily. The Erwin pottery specializes in an under-glazed, hand-painted dinnerware.

Excepts from "White, Granite & Semi-Porcelain Wage Scale & Size List Agreement" between National Brotherhood of Operative Potters and The United States Potters Association. February, 1942:

Wages: Color Room – Male Dippers, when dipping – $.765 per hour
Female Dippers, when dipping – $.585 per hour
(Even then there was a difference in men's and women's wages!)

Slip Tinting – Male: $.77 per hour; Female: $.55 per hour

Handling: The employer may require that all handles be cut and stuck on by the handler. All handles shall be finished inside and outside and properly trimmed, and the boxing of cups must be done by the handler.

Jiggering: The jiggerman was very important. He hired his own crew, which for hollow ware consists of a mould runner and a baller and the total pay was divided among them as follows: Jiggerman – 50.25% Mould runner – 26.75% and Baller: 23.00%

For mixing bowls – $.0964 per doz.
Cups – $.0474 per doz.
Sugars – ordinary – $.4743 per dozen

Flatware crews consisted of the Jiggerman, Battersout and Mould Runner. They divided pay as follows: Jiggerman – 44.33%, Battersout – 29.06%, and Mould runner – 26.61%

Fruits – $.9712 per doz.
Coupe Soup – $.1210 per doz.
Plate, 8" – $.1198 per doz.

Maintenance men – $.75 per hour.
Tunnel Kiln Firemen – $.94 per hour.
Journeyman Warehousemen – $.88 per hour.
Minimum rates – Male, $.68 per hour; Female, $.515 per hour.

Pressing: Clay to be delivered by the firm to floor on which it is used free of charge. One-third shall be deducted from price of a footed article when same is made without foot. One-half of the price of an unfooted article shall be added when same is made with foot.

Packers: Salary – $1.05 per hour.

Packers used crates, boxes, and barrels or casks. Packed with straw: "On all casks that will weigh 500# or more when packed, every stave must be nailed through both bilge hoops. Liners must be put on all casks larger than a #5. The locks of the quarter or under head hoops must be securely nailed."

"No two or more pieces shall be packed together without straw between them. Unless they are wrapped in paper, the bodies and covers of Sugars and Teapots shall be separated with straw."

"In setting prices for packing new strawless cartons, the Standing committee shall use the past six weeks average hourly earnings at packing strawless cartons as a basis for settlement."
24 pc. — $.0517   41 pc. — $.0808   50 pc. — $.1121

Turners: "Turners must see that all edges of cups and bowls are finished round and smooth, and all sharp edges eliminated. When the turner is in doubt as to greenware being in a proper state of dryness to produce perfect work, and to permit handles to be attached securely, he shall not turn such ware without consent of the firm. The use of two tools at one time by a turner is strictly forbidden and no turner shall at any time attempt to top and polish or top and burnish at the same."

"Where Liners do back numbering, they shall not number more than one piece in a set of twenty pieces or more."
This may explain why so few pieces are found with pattern numbers.

Decal Prices: size 2 – 2⅞" – $.0446 per dozen
Single side sprays – $.0535 per dozen. Semi-border and center – $.1782 per dozen.

After reading this entire book, only a very small part of which is listed herein, we feel that compiling the payroll in a pottery must have been a nightmare!

PHOTOGRAPHING YOUR COLLECTION

Various cameras can be used to photograph your Blue Ridge. While 35mm is most common, larger formats can be even better if you have one and know how to use it. Of the more common cameras, 35mm single lens reflex (SLR) is best, but many point-and-shoot models are OK. A single lens reflex need not be the latest, most expensive model. A 20-year-old Pentax K-1000 with a reasonably good lens will serve as well as a $1,700.00 Nikon F4S. Point-and-shoot cameras with close focusing ability can work well.

Backgrounds should help separate and delineate the pieces. They should be plain, smooth, and seamless. Avoid black or white; colors of medium tones are best. Several things work well as background, such as cheap poster board, window shades, cloth (no wrinkles), and plush carpet. Photo stores sell rolls of paper in many colors and different widths for this specific purpose. In the vertical position, the backdrop should be hung so that it curves smoothly forward to provide a floor for the piece. There should be no visible line where the material curves forward. The simplest method of creating a smooth background is to lay the material flat. The camera position is then more or less directly over the subject.

Lighting can be very simple by making use of the sun. On a clear day, open shade provides a very nice light. A day which is cloudy but bright is also good. Place your set-up out in the open. During a photo session for one of our books, we worked inside a garage. The weather was clear and bright and by simply leaving the door open we had a very nice light to work with. (As I remember it, we also had a couple of inquisitive bumblebees hanging around, but that's neither here nor there.) For working indoors, photo floodlights are the easiest to use. Two bowl-shaped reflectors equipped with clamps are adequate. These lights should be fitted with No. 1 blue bulbs (250 watt) available at most camera stores. The light from household bulbs is very yellow and is difficult for even a custom photo lab to correct. No. 1 blue Foto Flood bulbs unfortunately cost about $3.50 each and last about 3 hours. You can greatly extend their lives by turning them on only for a final viewfinder check of each setup and then off after the exposure is taken.

Camera-mounted flash can be used with care. Place plates directly on the background laid on the floor. Take one exposure from directly over the pieces; back up a little way and take a second exposure; take a third from a little more of an angle and select the finished print that shows the best detail and the least amount of flare. ("Flare" is the light spots from flash, which blots out part of the pattern.)

If you use a SLR camera, use the manual mode. Take a light reading with an incident light meter or use the camera's built-in meter reading from a Kodak 18% Gray Card (available from most camera stores). Once you have set the exposure, do not change it as long as light conditions remain the same.

With a point-and-shoot camera, you must rely on the auto exposure feature of the camera even if it does not always produce the best picture. Also keep in mind that the viewfinder of these cameras is offset from the lens and in close-up photos, what you see is not what you get. If you center the object in the viewfinder, it will appear in the lower corner of the print, likely partially cut off. This problem is called "parallax." Many point-and-shoot cameras have close-focus frame lines show in the viewfinder. These lines are helpful but not a sure thing. Observation and experience are your best guides. Allowing a little extra margin around the object can be good insurance,

When using photo floodlights, a sturdy tripod is a great help. If you do not have one, borrow or, if necessary, rent one. You will be well pleased with the result. Using a cable release or the self-timer will keep the camera steadier. I have several tripods that I use for different occasions; a solid elevator tripod for studio and general use, a lightweight one to carry around, and a heavy monster for my largest camera and special uses.

Of the readily available films, I consider Kodak Gold 400 or Fuji 400 print film the best. Some photographers will argue for a slower film. Their reasons are valid for slides or big enlargements, but for prints of 8" x 10" or smaller, the advantages of faster films far outweigh the drawbacks. The higher speed rating will allow higher shutter speeds and smaller lens openings, both of which will result in sharper pictures. Fast films also reduce the need for flash in your general photography.

Processing the film may take some judgment on the part of the photographer. One-hour developers not only are the most expensive, but also the least likely to produce satisfactory results. Other 24 or 48 hours services can be variable. Some are usually quite good while others are often poor. If the processor you presently use gives you consistently good, clear prints with proper color balance, stay with it. Some of the mail-order processors provide very good work at low prices. Clark Color Laboratories (P.O. Box 96300, Washington, D.C. 20090) is an excellent example.

We hope all of this will help you take really glorious photos of your collection, and we also hope you will share them with us.

— *Bill Newbound*

SOUTHERN POTTERIES MARKS

In the beginning (1917–1923) Southern Potteries produced decal and transfer decorated dinnerware under the name Clinchfield Pottery. (See the Clinchfield Pottery section of this book for marks used during this time period.)

The name Blue Ridge was introduced about 1932 or 1933. Unfortunately, there are no surviving records to tell us when the various marks were used. In fact, there were periods when several marks were used simultaneously. We know the "Blue Ridge, China" mark was used after 1945, because that was the time when china pieces were first introduced. Also, the marks using the words "detergent proof" and "oven safe" were used in the later years.

Underglaze
Hand Painted
S.P. Inc.
Erwin, Tenn.
Oven Proof

Underglaze
Hand Painted
Made Especially for
Blair

SOUTHERN HAND PAINTED
MADE
ERWIN, TENN.
© THREE LITTLE PIGS
WALT E. DISNEY
U.S.A
CLINCHFIELD WARE.

Oven Proof
Underglaze
Hand Painted
Southern Potteries
MADE IN
U. S. A.

Blue Ridge
China
Hand Painted
Underglaze
Southern Potteries, Inc.
MADE IN U. S. A.

HAND PAINTED
UNDER THE
GLAZE
Southern
MADE
IN U.S.A.
OVEN PROOF
FADE PROOF

Blue Ridge
Hand Painted
Underglaze
Southern Potteries, Inc.
MADE IN U. S. A.
10D

Underglaze
Hand Painted
S.P. Inc.
Erwin, Tenn.

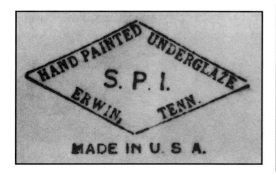

HAND PAINTED UNDERGLAZE
S. P. I.
ERWIN, TENN.
MADE IN U.S.A.

"Countryside"

HAND PAINTED

UNDERGLAZE

SOUTHERN POTTERIES, INC.

MADE IN U.S.A.

SOUTHERN
POTTERIES, INC.
ERWIN, TENN.

**This mark found on
animal figures.**

This mark is often found on restaurant ware and is <u>not</u> Southern Potteries.

Although Southern did make some things for Fondeville, this mark is found on items that are <u>not</u> Southern Potteries.

THE JOBBER JUMBLE

There has been some confusion regarding the various jobber marks used in Southern Potteries products, especially in the case of the PV in a circle. First of all, keep in mind that a jobber or wholesaler buys merchandise for resale from many different manufacturers, sometimes having the jobber's own mark applied to the product, and sometimes not.

The PV mark stands for "Peasant Village" which was a trademark used by Mittledorfer Straus, Inc. of New York City. Southern Potteries did many items for Peasant Village, but so did other potteries. Just because an item is marked PV does not mean it is a Southern Potteries product. You have to pay strict attention to whether the item is on a Southern blank or shape; whether it is hand painted under the glaze; whether, indeed, it "looks Southern."

The French Opera plate series marked PV that turns up here and there is a good example of how confusing reproductions and marks can be. As I understand it, the original series of plates were late 19th century European products. Around the time of World War II when imports were cut off, Mittledorfer Straus had the plates made in this country and marked with the PV symbol. The same plates were also made by Vernon Kilns in California and scribed with *their* marks and an explanation that they were reproductions.

Another jobber mark that is often seen on Southern Potteries products and also on Japanese ware is the UCAGO (United China and Glass Company) logo. In fact, I understand this is the company that at one point took Blue Ridge to Japan and had it reproduced. Check your UCAGO mark and be sure it is "Made in U.S.A." and not Japan.

A mark we have sometimes found on boots is the Ebeling and Rauss Company of Devon and later Royersford, Pennsylvania. This mark will often be found with a drawing of a bell incorporated into it. Ebeling and Rauss went bankrupt in the mid 1980s, I understand, and all records were disposed of. They are now back in business in Allentown, Pennsylvania, having been purchased by Ronald Rapelje in 1992. They are strictly a wholesaler for the gift shop trade; they do not make any pottery themselves.

The Stanhome Ivy pattern has confused a lot of folks because you can find three different marks on the same pattern and shape. There is the special Stanhome mark, the Blue Ridge mark, and the Cannonsburg mark. This was a puzzler, but we have discovered the reason for the Cannonsburg mark. It seems that after Southern Potteries closed, a group of the decorators moved to the Cannonsburg Pottery and for over a year, painted the Stanhome Ivy pattern — and others — for Cannonsburg. Thus the three different marks. Only the Stanhome mark or the Blue Ridge mark is actually a Southern Potteries product. See the Marks Section in this book for other jobbers that bought from Southern Potteries.

JOBBERS' MARKS

Jobber marks were used by the many, many smaller firms who sold wholesale and/or retail to their own clientele and who ordered merchandise from Southern Potteries among others. They usually wanted these products marked with their own logo. Please keep in mind that all the marks we show here are taken from verified pieces of Southern Potteries manufacture. How-ever, this does not mean that everything you might find marked with a certain jobber's logo was made by Southern Potteries! Jobbers ordered from many sources and even other countries, so you have to know your Southern Potteries patterns, colors and especially shapes in order to conclude that a certain piece is indeed Blue Ridge dinnerware.

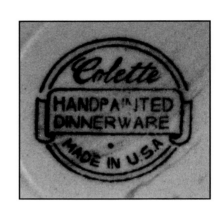

BERKSHIRE
Underglaze
Hand Painted
MADE IN U. S. A.

BEVERLEY
Underglaze
Hand Painted
MADE IN U. S. A.

BLUE WILLOW
UNDERGLAZE
A FRANKLIN KENT
CREATION
MADE IN U. S. A.

Sunshine
Hand Painted
Dinnerware
MADE IN U.S.A.

American Home
Genuine China

Mount Vernon
Hand Painted
UNDERGLAZE
MADE iN U.S.A.

TULIP
Underglaze
Hand Painted
MADE IN U.S.A.

MOUNTAIN CRAB
BLUE RIDGE MOUNTAINS
HAND ART

VALLEY BLOSSOM
BLUE RIDGE MOUNTAINS
HAND ART

VITAMIN FROLICS
CLINCHFIELD
BLUE RIDGE MOUNTAINS
HAND ART

Underglaze
Hand Painted
MADE IN
U.S.A.
LAUREL WREATH

"Royal"
OVEN WARE
GUARANTEED 100%
OVEN PROOF
MADE IN
U. S. A.

OVENPROOF
PRIMROSE

SUN CHINA CO.
MADE IN U. S. A.
WARRANTED
22 KT. GOLD

RED LEAF
HAND PAINTED
UNDERGLAZE
MADE IN U.S.A.

R. H E. Co.
2244-U
UNION MADE
IN U.S.A.

P.V.

Good Housekeeping
Genuine China

KING's
HAND PAINTED
UNDERGLAZE
MADE IN U.S.A.

WESTWOOD
Underglaze
Hand Painted
MADE IN U.S.A.

FONDEVILLE
NEW YORK

Chicago
Underglaze
Hand Painted
U.S.A.

Charm House
FIVE   C&G   HAND
CHINA   PAINTED

NASCO
Underglaze
Hand Painted
MADE IN
U.S.A.

PRICE GUIDE

Do we really need to mention that this listing of prices should be considered a guide, not a Bible? We see unbelievable prices advertised here and there and in shops and malls but remember the old saying "Askin' ain't gettin'." We try to gather "sold at" prices from various parts of the country and then average them in order to get a good idea of actual sales prices.

Prices listed are for items in perfect condition; no cracks, chips, browning or large amounts of crazing. We list a range in prices, with the simple patterns at the low end and the more elaborate patterns at the top. China (porcelain) and earthenware prices are listed separately for pieces that were made both ways. Some bodies and lids are also listed separately.

Premium patterns include those with people, barns, houses, roosters, chickens, animals, birds, home interiors, holiday motifs, Mexican and Oriental motifs, pixies, wallpaper patterns, and designer plates, which are fanciful and outrageous but were never placed on the market.

Ashtrays, Individual..$18.00–22.00
Ashtrays, Advertising, railroad $60.00–75.00
Ashtrays, Advertising, round $45.00–50.00
Ashtrays with rest (eared) $20.00–25.00
Ashtray, Mallard Box shape........................$35.00–40.00
Basket, 10" Aluminum edge $25.00–30.00
Basket, 7" Aluminum edge $18.00–25.00
Bon-bon, Charm House, china..................$95.00–125.00
Bon-bon, div. ctr. hdl, china $85.00–95.00
Bon-bon, Flat shell, china............................$65.00–75.00
Bon-bon, Flat shell, Pixie, china $95.00–100.00
Bowl, 5¼" fruit..$6.00–8.00
Bowl, 6" cereal/soup.....................................$10.00–12.00
Bowl, 6" cereal/soup, Premium $20.00–25.00
Bowl, Flat soup $12.00–15.00
Bowl, Flat soup, Premium $25.00–30.00
Bowl, Hot cereal $10.00–12.00
Bowl, 10½"–11½" Salad $60.00–70.00
Bowl, 11½" Square Dancers $125.00–150.00
Bowl, cov. vegetable......................................$50.00–60.00
Bowl, cov. veg., Premium $95.00–125.00
Bowl, Mixing, small $15.00–20.00
Bowl, Mixing, medium $20.00–25.00
Bowl, Mixing, large $25.00–30.00
Bowl, 8" round veg..$15.00–20.00

Bowl, 9" oval veg..$20.00–25.00
Bowl, 9" oval veg. divided $20.00–25.00
Box, 6" rd. Cov. candy, china $135.00–150.00
Box, Sq. cigarette only...................................$60.00–70.00
Box, Dancing Nudes, china $500.00–750.00
Box, Mallard Duck $600.00–700.00
Box, Round cov. powder $150.00–175.00
Box, Rose Step, china...................................$150.00–160.00
Box, Rose Step, pearlized.............................$70.00–80.00
Box, Seaside, china $150.00–170.00
Box, Seaside w/ashtrays $200.00–250.00
Box, Sherman Lily $700.00–800.00
Breakfast set $400.00–450.00
Breakfast set, Premium,............................$550.00–600.00
Butterdish $35.00–40.00
Butterdish, Woodcrest $45.00–50.00
Butterpat/Coaster $30.00–35.00
Cake lifter $25.00–30.00
Cake tray, Maple Leaf, china $60.00–65.00
Carafe, w/lid $95.00–125.00
Casserole, w/lid $40.00–50.00
Celery, Leaf shape, china.............................$45.00–55.00
Celery, Skyline $25.00–35.00
Child's cereal bowl $85.00–95.00
Child's mug..$75.00–85.00

Child's plate $95.00–120.00

Child's feeding dish, div. $120.00–150.00

Child's Play Tea Set $350.00–375.00

Chocolate pot...............................$200.00–225.00

Chocolate tray $400.00–450.00

Coffee Pot, ovoid shape $115.00–125.00

Counter sign $300.00–350.00

Creamer, regular shapes $12.00–15.00

Creamer, Charm House $65.00–85.00

Creamer, pedestal, china $50.00–60.00

Creamer, demi, china $65.00–75.00

Creamer, demi, earthenware.........$35.00–40.00

Creamer, Fifties shape $10.00–15.00

Creamer, Rope Handle $10.00–15.00

Creamer, sm. Colonial, open.........$10.00–15.00

Creamer, lg. Colonial, open $15.00–18.00

Creamer, Waffle shape..................$12.00–15.00

Cup & Saucer, demi, china...........$35.00–45.00

Cup & Saucer, demi, Premium.....$50.00–60.00

Cup & Saucer, Jumbo $55.00–65.00

Cup & Saucer, regular shapes $12.00–15.00

Cup & Saucer, Premium...............$50.00–60.00

Cup & Saucer, demi, earthenware $25.00–30.00

Cup & Saucer, Holiday.................$50.00–65.00

Cup & Saucer, artist-signed.........$400.00–450.00

Custard cup $10.00–14.00

Demi Pot, china............................$150.00–180.00

Demi Pot, earthenware..................$100.00–110.00

Dish, 8 x 13" baking, divided $25.00–30.00

Dish, 8 x 13" baking, plain $20.00–25.00

Dish, 8 x 13" baking w/metal stand $35.00–40.00

Egg cup, double $25.00–30.00

Egg cup, Premium $50.00–55.00

Egg dish, deviled..........................$50.00–60.00

Glass, tumbler $12.00–15.00

Glass, dessert cup.........................$10.00–12.00

Glass, juice tumbler......................$12.00–15.00

Gravy Boat $20.00–25.00

Gravy Boat, Premium....................$50.00–55.00

Gravy tray $25.00–30.00

Jug, Character, Pioneer Woman.............$500.00–575.00

Jug, Character, Daniel Boone.................$700.00–750.00

Jug, Character, Indian...............$700.00–750.00

Jug, Character, Paul Revere $700.00–750.00

Jug, Batter w/lid $75.00–85.00

Jug, Syrup w/lid $85.00–95.00

Lamp, china................................$200.00–250.00

Lamp from pitcher, teapot, etc. $60.00–75.00

Lazy Susan complete $650.00–700.00

Lazy Susan, center bowl w/lid $150.00–160.00

Lazy Susan, side pieces...............$85.00–90.00

Lazy Susan, wooden base..........$80.00–85.00

Leftover, sm. w/lid.....................$18.00–22.00

Leftover, med. w/lid $20.00–25.00

Leftover, lg. w/lid $25.00–35.00

Marmite w/lid, Charm House $150.00–170.00

Pie baker.....................................$25.00–35.00

Pitcher, Abby, china...................$150.00–175.00

Pitcher, Abby, earthenware $60.00–70.00

Pitcher, Alice, 6¼" earthenware $85.00–95.00

Pitcher, Alice 6", china...............$150.00–175.00

Pitcher, Antique, 5", china $75.00–85.00

Pitcher, Antique, 3½"..................$150.00–175.00

Pitcher, Betsy, china....................$175.00–195.00

Pitcher, Betsy, earthenware $85.00–95.00

Pitcher, Betsy, gold decorated $300.00–325.00

Pitcher, Charm House $190.00–220.00

Pitcher, Chick, china...................$95.00–110.00

Pitcher, Clara, china....................$85.00–95.00

Pitcher, Grace, china...................$85.00–95.00

Pitcher, Helen, china ....$85.00 - 95.00

Pitcher, Jane, china $110.00–125.00

Pitcher, Martha, earthenware.......$70.00–75.00

Pitcher, Milady, china $150.00–190.00

Pitcher, Rebecca $150.00–195.00

Pitcher, Sally, china.....................$175.00–195.00

Pitcher, Sculptured Fruit, china...............$85.00–90.00

Pitcher, Sculptured Fruit, Petite $80.00–85.00

Pitcher, 7" Spiral, earthenware...............$50.00–70.00

Pitcher, 7" Spiral, china $80.00–85.00

Pitcher, 7" Spiral, Premium $100.00–125.00

Pitcher, 4¼" Spiral, china $150.00–200.00

Pitcher, 6½" Virginia, china........$80.00–95.00

Pitcher, 4¼" Virginia, china........$150.00–190.00

Pitcher, Watauga $350.00–400.00

Plate, Advertising, lg. $375.00–450.00

Plate, artist-signed, 10" $575.00–600.00

Plate, artist-signed, Gold Cabin $600.00–675.00

Plate, artist-signed, Quail $600.00–625.00

Plate, artist-signed, Turkey Gobbler.........$900.00–975.00

Plate, 12", aluminum edge $40.00–45.00

Plate, 14", Square Dance........................$200.00–250.00

Plate, 11½"–12" $35.00–40.00

Plate, 11½"–12", Premium.........................$100.00–125.00

Plate, 10½" dinner.................................$15.00–22.00

Plate, 10½" dinner, Premium........................$50.00–60.00

Plate, 9¼" dinner.................................$15.00–20.00

Plate, 9¼" dinner, Premium.........................$40.00–45.00

Plate, divided $30.00–35.00

Plate, heavy divided $35.00–40.00

Plate, party w/cup well & cup $25.00–35.00

Plate, party w/cup well & cup, Premium......$60.00–75.00

Plate 8" sq. $15.00–20.00

Plate, 8" Square Dancers (square or round) ..$75.00–80.00

Plate, 7" round....................................$8.00–12.00

Plate, 7" square...................................$12.00–15.00

Plate 6" round.....................................$6.00–8.00

Plate, 6" square (novelty patterns)..............$65.00–75.00

Plate, 6" square, Provincial Farm scenes......$75.00–80.00

Plate, 8½" Bird salad $75.00–80.00

Plate, 8½" Flower or fruit salad..................$20.00–25.00

Plate, 8½" Still Life...............................$25.00–30.00

Plate, 8½" Language of Flowers $75.00–85.00

Plate, 11" Specialty $100.00–125.00

Plate, Designer....................................$95.00–100.00

Plate, Christmas Tree................................$65.00–75.00

Plate, Christmas Doorway $80.00–85.00

Plate, Thanksgiving Turkey $80.00–85.00

Plate, Turkey w/acorns $85.00–90.00

Platter, artist-signed, 15"......................$900.00–975.00

Platter, Turkey patterns $240.00–250.00

Platter, 15" regular patterns.........................$30.00–35.00

Platters, 12½", 13"..................................$18.00–22.00

Platters, Premium` ....add 25–30%

Ramekin, 5" w/lid $25.00–30.00

Ramekin, 7½" w/lid $35.00–40.00

Relish, Charm House................................$125.00–150.00

Relish, deep shell, china..............................$70.00–85.00

Relish, Heart shape................................$80.00–90.00

Relish, individual, Crescent shape $20.00–25.00

Relish, Loop Handle, china $75.00–85.00

Relish, Palisades..................................$50.00–60.00

Relish, Mod Leaf, china $65.00–70.00

Relish, T-handle $65.00–70.00

Salad Fork, china $40.00–50.00

Salad Spoon, china.................................$40.00–50.00

Salad Fork, Earthenware $35.00–40.00

Sconce, wall $70.00–75.00

Server, wood or metal ctr. handle $20.00–25.00

Shakers, 1¾" Apple, pair $25.00–30.00

Shakers, 2¼" Apple, pair $35.00–40.00

Shakers, 1¾" Apple w/floral, pair $30.00–35.00

Shakers, Blossom Top, pair $45.00–50.00

Shakers, Bud Top, pair $45.00–50.00

Shakers, Charm House, pair $125.00–150.00

Shakers, Chickens, pair $125.00–150.00

Shakers, Good Housekeeping, pair $90.00–95.00

Shakers, Range, pair $40.00–45.00

Shakers, Mallards, pair............................$325.00–350.00

Shakers, Palisades, pair $20.00–25.00

Shakers, tall footed, china, pair.....................$70.00–80.00

Shakers, Skyline, pair $20.00–25.00

Sherbet..$22.00–25.00

Sugar, Charm House................................$65.00–75.00

Sugar, Colonial, eared, open.........................$15.00–20.00

Sugar, Colonial, small, open $15.00–18.00

Sugar, Pedestal, china $50.00–60.00

Sugar, regular shapes w/lid.........................$15.00–20.00

Sugar, Rope Handle, w/lid..........................$18.00 - 20.00

Sugar, Square Round, w/lid $18.00–20.00

Sugar, Waffle, w/lid...............................$18.00–20.00

Sugar, Woodcrest, w/lid............................$18.00–20.00

Tea Tile, 6" round or square $45.00–60.00

Tea Tile, 3" round or square $35.00–45.00

Teapot, Ball shape $125.00–150.00

Teapot, Ball shape, Premium....................$200.00–225.00

Teapot, Charm House $250.00–300.00

Teapot, Chevron handle.............................$150.00–165.00

Teapot, Colonial $95.00–125.00

Teapot, Fine Panel, china $140.00–150.00

Teapot, Good Housekeeping, china $160.00–175.00

Teapot, Mini Ball, china $150.00–200.00

Teapot, Palisades $90.00–100.00

Teapot, Piecrust.....................................$95.00–100.00

Teapot, Rope Handle $85.00–95.00

Teapot, Skyline...$75.00–85.00

Teapot, Snub Nose, china.........................$170.00–185.00

Teapot, Square Round, 7".........................$90.00–100.00

Teapot, Square Round, 6"...........................$95.00–110.00

Teapot, Woodcrest $125.00–150.00

Tidbit, 2-tier..$20.00–25.00

Tidbit, 3-tier..$25.00–35.00

Toast, covered..$110.00–125.00

Toast, covered, Premium $185.00–200.00

Toast, covered, French Peasant.................$200.00–225.00

Toast, lid only, Premium & Peasant..........$110.00–125.00

Toast, lid only, regular $65.00–75.00

Tray, demi, Colonial, 5½" x 7"..................$120.00–140.00

Tray, demi, Colonial, French Peasant $210.00–225.00

Tray, demi, Skyline 9½" x 7⅝"......................$80.00–95.00

Tray, snack, Martha $150.00–160.00

Tray, Waffle set, 9½" x 13½".....................$95.00–110.00

Vase, bud $140.00–160.00

Vase, Tapered, china $95.00–110.00

Vase, handled, china....................................$90.00–95.00

Vase, 8" boot $90.00–95.00

Vase, 9½" ruffle top, china $90.00–95.00

INDEX

COLLECTOR BOOKS

Informing Today's Collector

For over two decades we have been keeping collectors informed on trends and values in all fields of antiques and collectibles.

The following is a partial listing of our books on pottery, porcelain, and figurines:

American Limoges-Limoges-8½x11-208 Pgs.-(HB) ....#4630/$24.95

Blue and White Stoneware-McNerney-5½x8½-152 Pgs.-(PB).....................#1312/$ 9.95

Blue Ridge Dinnerware, Revised 3rd Ed.-Newbound-8½x11-160 Pgs.-(PB)........#1958/$14.95

Blue Willow, Revised 2nd Ed.-Gaston-8½x11-169 Pgs.-(HB) ....#1959/$14.95

Collectible **Vernon Kilns**-Nelson-8½x11-256 Pgs.-(HB) ....#3816/$24.95

Collecting **Yellow Ware**-McAllister-8½x11-128 Pgs.-(HB) ....#3311/$16.95

Collector's Ency. of **American Dinnerware**-Cunningham-8½x11-322 Pgs.-(HB) ...#1373/$24.95

Collector's Ency. of **Blue Ridge Dinnerware**-Newbound-8½x11-176 Pgs.-(HB)...#3815/$19.95

Collector's Ency. of **Brush-McCoy Pottery**-Huxford-8½x11-192 Pgs.-(HB) .....#4658/$24.95

Collector's Ency. of **California Pottery**-Chipman-8½x11-160 Pgs.-(HB) ....#2272/$24.95

Collector's Ency. of **Colorado Pottery**-Carlton-8½x11-168 Pgs.-(HB) ....#3811/$24.95

Collector's Ency. of **Cookie Jars**-Roerig-8½x11-312 Pgs.-(HB) ....#2133/$24.95

Collector's Ency. of **Cookie Jars**, Vol II-Roerig-8½x11-400 Pgs-(HB) ....#3723/$24.95

Collector's Ency. of **Cowan Pottery**-Saloff-8½x11-176 Pgs.-(HB) ....#3429/$24.95

Collector's Ency. of **Dakota Potteries**-Dommel-8½x11-176 Pgs.-(HB) ....#4638/$24.95

Collector's Ency. of **Early Noritake**-Alden-8½x11-216 Pgs.-(HB) ....#3961/$24.95

Collector's Ency. of **Fiesta**-Huxford-8½x11-190 Pgs.-(HB) ....#2209/$19.95

Collector's Ency. of **Figural Planters & Vases**-Newbound-8½x11-232 Pgs.-(HB) ...#4718/$19.95

Collector's Ency. of **Flow Blue China**-Gaston-8½x11-160 Pgs.-(HB) ....#1439/$19.95

Collector's Ency. of **Flow Blue China**, 2nd Edition-Gaston-8½x11-184 Pgs.-(HB) ...#3812/$24.95

Collector's Ency. of **Hall China**, 2nd Edition-Whitmyer-8½x11-272 Pgs.-(HB) ...#3813/$24.95

Collector's Ency. of **Homer Laughlin China**-Jasper-8½x11-208 Pgs.-(HB) .....#3431/$24.95

Collector's Ency. of **Hull Pottery**-Roberts-8½x11-207 Pgs.-(HB) ....#1276/$19.95

Collector's Ency. of **Knowles, Taylor & Knowles China**-Gaston-8½x11-176 Pgs.-(HB)....#4573/$24.95

Collector's Ency. of **Lefton China**-DeLozier-8½x11-144 Pgs.-(HB) ....#3962/$19.95

Collector's Ency. of **Limoges Porcelain**, 2nd Ed.-Gaston-8½x11-224 Pgs.-(HB) ...#2210/$24.95

Collector's Ency. of **Majolica**-Katz-Marks-8½x11-192 Pgs.-(HB) ....#2334/$19.95

Collector's Ency. of **McCoy Pottery**-Huxford-8½x11-247 Pgs.-(HB) ....#1358/$19.95

Collector's Ency. of **Metlox** Potteries-Gibbs-8½x11-344 Pgs.-(HB) ....#3963/$24.95

Collector's Ency. of **Niolak**-Gifford-8½x11-256 Pgs.-(HB) ....#3313/$19.95

Collector's Ency. of **Nippon Porcelain** I-Van Patten-8½x11-222 Pgs.-(HB) ...#3837/$24.95

Collector's Ency. of **Nippon Porcelain**, 2nd Series-Van Patten-8½x11-256 Pgs.-(HB)........#2089/$24.95

Collector's Ency. of **Nippon Porcelain**, 3rd Series-Van Patten-8½x11-320 Pgs.-(HB) ....#1665/$24.95

Collector's Ency. of **Noritake**-Van Patten-8½x11-200 Pgs.-(HB) ....#1447/$19.95

Collector's Ency. of **Noritake**, 2nd Series-Van Patten-8½x11-264 Pgs.-(HB) ...#3432/$24.95

Collector's Ency. of **Occupied Japan**, Vol. I-Florence-8½x11-108 Pgs.-(PB) ...#1037/$14.95

Collector's Ency. of **Occupied Japan**, Vol. II-Florence-8½x11-112 Pgs.-(PB) ...#1038/$14.95

Collector's Ency. of **Occupied Japan**, Vol. III-Florence-8½x11-144 Pgs.-(PB) ...#2088/$14.95

Collector's Ency. of **Occupied Japan**, Vol. IV-Florence-8½x11-128 Pgs.-(PB) ...#2019/$14.95

Collector's Ency. of **Occupied Japan**, Vol. V-Florence-8½x11-128 Pgs.-(PB) ...#2335/$14.95

Collector's Ency. of **Pickard China**-Reed-8½x11-336 Pgs.-(HB) ....#3964/$24.95

Collector's Ency. of **R.S. Prussia**, 1st Series-Gaston-8½x11-216 Pgs.-(HB) ...#1311/$24.95

Collector's Ency. of **R.S. Prussia**, 2nd Series-Gaston-8½x11-230 Pgs.-(HB) ...#1715/$24.95

Collector's Ency. of **R.S. Prussia**, 3rd Series-Gaston-8½x11-224 Pgs.-(HB) ...#3726/$24.95

Collector's Ency. of **R.S. Prussia**, 4th Series-Gaston-8½x11-288 Pgs.-(HB) ...#3877/$24.95

Collector's Ency. of **Roseville Pottery**-Huxford-8½x11-192 Pgs.-(HB) ....#1034/$19.95

Collector's Ency. of **Roseville Pottery**, Vol. 2-Huxford-8½x11-207 Pgs.-(HB) ...#1035/$19.95

Collector's Ency. of **Sascha Brastoff**-Conti, Bethany, Seay-8½x11-320 Pgs.-(HB)...............#3965/$24.95

Collector's Ency. of **Van Briggle** Art Pottery-Sasicki & Fania-8½x11-144 Pgs.-(HB) ....#3314/$24.95

Collector's Ency. of **Wall Pockets**-Newbound-8½x11-192 Pgs.-(HB) ....#4563/$19.95

Collector's Ency. of **Weller Pottery**-Huxford-8½x11-376 Pgs.-(HB) ....#2111/$29.95

Collector's Guide to **Country Stoneware & Pottery**-Raycraft-5½x8½-160 Pgs.-(PB)...........#3452/$11.95

Collector's Guide to **Country Stoneware & Pottery**, 2nd Series-Raycraft-8½x11-375 Pgs-(PB)...#2077/$14.95

Collector's Guide to **Hull Pottery**, The Dinnerware Lines-Gick-Burke-8½x11-168 Pgs.-(PB).....#3434/$16.95

Collector's Guide to **Lu-Ray Pastels**-Meehan-8½x11-160 Pgs.-(PB) ....#3876/$18.95

Collector's Guide to **Made in Japan** Ceramics-White-8½x11-214 Pgs.-(PB) ...#3814/$18.95

Collector's Guide to **Made in Japan** Ceramics, Book II-White-8½x11-256 Pgs.-(PB) ....#4646/$18.95

Collector's Guide to **McCoy Pottery**-Hanson-Nissen-Hanson-8½x11-336 Pgs.-(HB) ....#4722/$19.95

Collector's Guide to **Rockingham**-Brewer-5½x8½-128 Pgs.-(PB) ....#4565/$14.95

Collector's Guide to **Shawnee Pottery**-Vanderbilt-8½x11-160 Pgs.-(HB) .....#2339/$19.95

Cookie Jars-Westfall-5½x8½-160 Pgs.-(PB) ....#1425/$ 9.95

Cookie Jars, Book II-Westfall-8½x11-256 Pgs.-(PB)..........................#3440/$19.95

Debolt's Dictionary of **American Pottery Marks**-DeBolt-8½x11-288 Pgs.-(PB) ...#3435/$17.95

Early Roseville-Huxford-5½x8½-72 Pgs.-(PB)................................#2076/$ 7.95

Head Vases-Cole-8½x11-142 Pgs.-(PB) ....#1917/$14.95

Lehner's Ency. of **U.S. Marks** on Pottery, Porcelain & Clay-Lehner-8½x11-636 Pgs.-(HB)...#2379/$24.95

Purinton Pottery-Morris-8½x11-272 Pgs.-(HB) ....#3825/$24.95

Red Wing Art Pottery-Dollen-8½x11-144 Pgs.-(PB) ....#4726/$19.95

Red Wing Collectibles-DePasquale-5½x8½-160 Pgs.-(PB) ....#1670/$ 9.95

Red Wing Stoneware-DePasquale-5½x8½-160 Pgs.-(PB) ....#1440/$ 9.95

Shawnee Pottery-Mangus-8½x11-256 Pgs.-(HB) ....#3738/$24.95

Turn of the Century **American Dinnerware**-Jasper-8½x11-256 Pgs.-(HB).........#4629/$24.95

Wall Pockets of the Past-Perkins-8½x11-160 Pgs.-(PB) ....#4572/$17.95

Watt Pottery Id. & Value Guide-Morris-8½x11-160 Pgs.-(HB) ....#3327/$19.95

This is only a partial listing of the books on antiques & collectibles that are available from Collector Books. All books are well illustrated and contain current values. Most of the these books are available from your local bookseller, antique dealer, or public library. If you are unable to locate certain titles in your area, you may order by mail from COLLECTOR BOOKS, P.O. Box 3009, Paducah, KY 42002-3009. Customers with Visa or MasterCard may phone in orders from 7:00–5:00 CST, Monday–Friday, Toll-Free 1-800-626-5420. Add $2.00 for postage for the first book ordered and $0.30 for each additional book. Include item number, title, and price when ordering. Allow 14 to 21 days for delivery.

WE CARRY MORE THAN 300 BOOKS ON ANTIQUES & COLLECTIBLES • SEND FOR A FREE, COMPLETE LISTING OF ALL OUR TITLES